Florence Merriam Bailey

My Summer in a Mormon Village.

Florence Merriam Bailey

My Summer in a Mormon Village.

ISBN/EAN: 9783743337749

Manufactured in Europe, USA, Canada, Australia, Japa

Cover: Foto ©ninafisch / pixelio.de

Manufactured and distributed by brebook publishing software (www.brebook.com)

Florence Merriam Bailey

My Summer in a Mormon Village.

CONTENTS.

		PAGE
I.	A Haven of Rest	1
II.	A Mother in Israel	11
III.	On the Mountain Side	19
IV.	Horseback Riding	30
V.	The Little Home under the Bench	53
VI.	Village Life	65
VII.	Flash Lights	79
VIII.	The Brownies	85
IX.	Grandma	88
X.	Doctrines of the Latter-Day Saints	108
XI.	The Practice of the Doctrines	115
XII.	Polygamy	124
XIII.	The Great Salt Lake	140
XIV.	Climbing the Wasatch with a Professor	147

MY SUMMER IN A MORMON VILLAGE.

I.

A HAVEN OF REST.

WHEN I tell people that I went from New York to spend the summer in Utah, they look at me with such polite amazement that I hurriedly explain my errand. My friend, an enthusiastic student of birds, after her summer of study in Ohio and Colorado, was looking for new worlds to conquer. I went with her for the birds and the climate, — the too little known climate of the dry elevated region between the Rockies and the Sierra Nevada, known to geographers as the "Great Basin" of America. Utah and Arizona have this basin climate and are the natural sanitariums of our continent, far surpassing the Adirondacks,

Florida, and California in elevation, dryness, and recuperative effect, — especially in pulmonary difficulties.

We had been advised to begin the summer on an island in the Great Salt Lake, because of the rare opportunities it was supposed to afford for the study of desert birds. But one of the owners whom we consulted said that, while we might like to see the herds of elk and buffalo planted there, really there was no place for ladies; and the trip to the island involved an all-night's sail on a sail-boat. We remembered in discomfiture that Salt Lake was large, and meekly accepted his substitution of a neighboring Mormon village.

Our interest in the Mormon problem began on the train. The occupants of the car divided themselves into the observed and the observers. My friend and I whispered to each other about an unconscious group of women traveling under the leadership of one dogged-looking man, only to find ourselves under the speculative scrutiny of another Eastern tourist.

Even on the train we began to feel the grateful influence of restful country life. From the windows we watched the quiet lake, the wayside flowers, and the sea-gulls, engaged in the surprising occupation of following the plow. At our station, a Western meadow-lark sang his sweet strain from a telegraph pole; we could hear blackbirds calling from the marshes.

We took the only wagon that met the train, and drove through the village. It was a typical Mormon village, one of a line of closely connected settlements running along the valley between the Wasatch and the great lake. The settlements, — with their elaborate system of irrigation, — when contrasted with isolated farms of the East, afford examples of Brigham Young's shrewd policy of centralization.

But we were more interested in village life than in Brigham Young, just then. Many of the streets were lined with locust-trees, whose white blossoms in June filled the air with their delicious fragrance. Under the trees ran mountain brooks, falling in white cascades down the hilly streets. Picturesque low stone houses were set back in bushy yards, each house with its orchard beside it, — delightful old overgrown orchards, in which the children played and calves grazed in the dappling sunlight.

Long houses with two or more front doors excited our whispered comment, though we learned afterward that a new front door did not always mean a new wife. Children were everywhere. Almost every house had its baby. The most attractive were the little maidens whose flaxen curls and blue eyes were half hidden within demure pink or blue Mormon sunbonnets.

We drove to the only boarding house in the town, and felt at home in Utah the moment we looked into the honest, motherly face of our landlady. She could board us, and took us next door to engage rooms. She called her neighbor "aunt," though they were of an age, and it soon came over us that we were to live in a Mormon family. As we shrank from every-day contact with the painful life of polygamy, we were relieved to find that our family numbered only mother and daughters.

"Our house" was one of the most attractive of the village. It was partly hidden from the street by its lilacs, blooming against the fence; its trees and rosebushes set in its well-kept lawn, — almost the only lawn in the village, — and the glimpse of its vine-covered piazza, bay-window, and one-story sloping roof brought cosy, homelike suggestions.

While we rested on the piazza after our long journey, enjoying the peaceful village atmosphere, a pair of chickadees came flitting about our trees, with as familiar manners and homelike tones as if they were the same little friends we had known in the East, and had come to welcome us. Two boys in blue jeans came riding a bay horse down the street, — bareback, and one behind the other, as we soon learned was the fashion in Utah. They had their hands full of flowers, gathered on the mountain for their mother. I asked them for a few to send East, and when I gave them five cents they looked surprised, and held the bunch out to me again, as if I had not had my money's worth. Another time I saw a boy riding up the street with nosegays at his horse's ears. But though the children loved flowers, the village surprised me by its lack of gardens, — perhaps I imagined that the women had not the heart for flowers.

Rumor said that our house had been the scene of a religious tragedy in the past, but its life ran peacefully now. The four women — mother and daughters — brewed and baked, and saw to their own vegetable garden, orchard, chickens, and cows. The brunt of the work was taken by the oldest daughter, a sweet-faced school-teacher. No work was too hard for her if she could spare her delicate mother; and her thoughtful care was truly touching.

Our life was a tranquil one. Our events were the blooming of a rosebush, or an episode of the henroost or barnyard. We seemed to have found a veritable haven of rest.

One morning the whole family assembled in the back yard to take off a brood of chickens. Two of the daughters dragged a hencoop from the barn, and we all followed the mother up on the fragrant hay-mow. By the dim light streaking in between the boards, we discovered the motherly old hen sitting in one corner, her wings spread protectingly over her brood. The mother picked the hen up in her arms, saying, when I exclaimed at its serenity, "Oh, she knows what I'm goin' to do;" and a daughter gathered up the downy balls in her apron.

For some time, whenever we appeared at the kitchen doorway, we were beset by the expectant rooster and his harem; and one day while sitting in the front yard, a young broiler calmly flew up on my knee.

When not out with my friend watching birds, or wandering about the country on horseback, I lived in the front yard. A delightful old-fashioned rocking-chair was brought out for me, and in this I basked in the sun, looking with delight on the pink clover blossoms, the lilacs, snowballs, and great looming rosebushes that gave color to our yard. When my friend's daughter joined us, she swung a hammock under the trees, and from it watched the humming-birds who haunted the trumpet vine growing over the piazza.

From the orchard side of our lawn, kept green by weekly watering from the irrigation ditches, came in turn the fragrance of strawberries, raspberries, and ripe peaches.

On the other side was a strip of pasture, where our two cows grazed; and in our uneventful life their proceedings took on great importance. The mother of the two would answer to no more feminine name than "Tom," and her sour, discontented expression proved that she "saw the world awry." But Daisy, her daughter, a gracefully built little creature with delicately modeled head and neck, had a gentle face and would answer to her name, following us about for clover.

When our sweet school-teacher was pushing the lawn mower, after tea, and we sat idly under the trees enjoying the smell of the newly cut grass, the cows came down to join the family party. We laughed at Daisy's expression of mingled fear and interest as she looked through the fence at the mysterious machine, scattering grass about it. The house mother raked up the new-mown hay, handing it over the fence to the eager cows, when Tom would swallow hers and crowd up for Daisy's. At this, the mother would rap her on the back with her rake, and we would all rise up and add our reproaches to the blows.

But one June day, Tom was driven up to the village mountain pasture, for the summer, and we thought Daisy would be relieved. But no! The affectionate little cow galloped up and down from one end of the yard to the other, mooing piteously. The next morning, when we looked out, to our amazement Tom stood licking Daisy's face! The old cow whom we had thought so greedy and unfeeling had escaped from the mountain and come home to her daughter.

But our yard did not have grass enough for two, and again Tom was sent away. The grief of poor Daisy was human. She followed the house mother about the yard forlornly, and, when I petted her, raised her head to smell wistfully over my cheek. Her sensitive face actually took on lines of sorrow.

A second time we looked out in the morning, to find Tom waiting to be let into the yard. I could hardly keep Daisy from rushing out to her when I opened the gate. But this time Tom, as if ashamed of her homesickness, pushed past her daughter, crowding up for her food in her old greedy way. Daisy looked so grieved I pitied her, but before long I was pleased to find mother and daughter in the pasture chewing their cud, side by side, Daisy's face looking as if her mother had been washing it. After that, for several months, no attempt was made to separate the poor creatures, and life ran smoothly in our haven of rest.

II.

A MOTHER IN ISRAEL.

From our house we went to breakfast by a short cut through the raspberry patch, fresh with dew, and so over a plank across the mountain brook that separated the two yards. Once within the gates our hearts warmed at sight of the smiling face of our landlady, a veritable "mother in Israel;" whose big heart held tenderness enough for the sorrows of a world, and protecting love enough to cover every child and shield all living creatures.

She "mothered" all who came in her way: under her hand man and beast fared alike. Before complaining summer boarders came, Shep, her devoted dog, and Tom, her cat, often begged for food at breakfast; while Topsy, her lame dove, walked about the room with the air of a privileged character, condescendingly picking up the crumbs we threw her. At tea, one evening, an old hen brought her brood upon the mother's door-sill. At last I thought I should hear a harsh word from her. But instead she called out quickly, in her most motherly tones, " Well, you did want something for them before they went to bed, did n't you ? " and hurried out to give them their supper.

When speaking of a man's maltreating his horse, she exclaimed indignantly, " I just feel worse to have a dumb brute suffer than a man." Talking about her cows, which she had " raised from calves," and which she talked to like children, she looked up at me with her big honest eyes, and said, " I 've gone without many a time to have enough to buy feed for them cows."

We thought that it was not the only time she had " gone without." Indeed, it never seemed to occur to her to spend anything on herself: her one thought and prayer was that she might have enough to pay her debts and help the poor. When the village band came to the house, she emptied her purse for the boys, and when remonstrated with said, with a beautiful look in her eyes, " I guess it 'll come back to me somehow."

She was too generous ever to make money. When a party came to dinner from the city, we thought it would be a help to her; but she so loaded down her table with good things for the young people, she barely covered her extra expenses. When one of her family of boarders went away, she made a feast for the last meal, sometimes working half the night to prepare it. If the boarder had shown any appreciation of the kindness lavished upon her, the dear mother served the meal with choking voice, having to rush away into her storeroom, her tender heart overcome by the thought of parting.

If a trip to the lake was proposed, she would get her husband to hitch up the farm wagon and take the whole family for a picnic, making room for some tired neighbor who had few outings. She enjoyed it all in her hearty way, and we were thankful to get her away from her cares; but she always gave us so many extra dainties, it became a pleasure she could ill afford.

With all her hard work she found time to provide special dishes for her invalids. "Just take that," she would urge. "I used to make it for a sick girl who was here, and it did her lots of good." And when the result of her motherly care began to show, she rejoiced over every added pound, exclaiming with beaming face, "Just see how much better she looks!"

At meals she bustled about, urging us to eat, and dispensing big pitchers of milk and great bowls of rich cream; and when the chairs were drawn back would ask anxiously of every wayfaring drummer, "Could you make a good meal?"

When asked what one owed her for dinner, she answered apologetically, "Twenty-five cents." A man who had overpaid her by a few nickels found the money waiting for him on his chance return six months later. When told, after being cheated by tramps, that she should require pay in advance, she replied conclusively, "I can't bear to." When a rough man came, mumbling something about "mines shut down," she hurried into her storeroom, and brought out a bag of food. If laughed at, she said simply, "I couldn't help it. I thought, 'Suppose my own folks was goin' round out of work,' — it's awful;" and she hurried out to refill the bread-plate.

If obliged to say to her grandchildren, "You can't come to dinner now," she hurried around the table, slipping cookies into their hands before they could get to the door.

She waited on us with aching feet rather than ask her "girl," and, when she did prefer a request, it was in a tone of apology. But if we hinted that the woman was lazy, she exclaimed in her hearty way, "Oh no, she's *real* good when I'm sick." Forced occasionally to speak of a fault-finding boarder, she declared, "I was ashamed of her. How *can* folks act so!"

Her good husband had her honest, unworldly face, with a frank, manly way and hearty hand-shake. He was a neighbor to advise with, and one who would put up a widow's fence without being asked. At table he sat on a bench against the wall, and in the intervals of refilling the bread-plate, " mother " would sit down by his side, and they would bandy jokes like boy and girl. When he teased too hard she would put her hand on his shoulder as she got up, exclaiming with laughing remonstrance, " Now, pa ! "

The " silver trouble " threw her husband out of work during the summer, and the one thought of " mother " was to keep the family together till the " bad times " were tided over. Though half sick, she sent away her " girl," and set about the work of two, saying bravely, " We 'll get along somehow." As the times grew harder and the general distress greater, her cry was for money " to help the poor ; " and she set about relieving them in earnest when winter came on.

But her usefulness was not limited to days of financial trouble. Unconsciously she was always at work helping the world along, with the power of her beautiful motherly spirit. Every one felt her influence. The frivolous girl became more womanly in her presence, the cynic grew genial under the warmth of her beaming smile, the weary mourner took heart from her cheery courage. Even the rough workingmen who stopped for a meal felt the strength of her womanliness, and said, "Yes, ma'am," to her most respectfully; while she called them all "boys," in her hearty, motherly way.

She had had five children, she told us, but had "lost two," — with a look in her eyes that I turned from. Her sorrows, however, had only served to make her heart softer and her sympathies quicker. Her kitchen was the resort of her neighbors, the village sick were gladdened by her presence, the lonely orphan found comfort in her motherly arms.

She was the mother confessor of the neighborhood. Though a Gentile, in the midst of Mormons, during the time when large rewards were offered for information of polygamous marriages, it was her ear in which the agonized wives told their tales of sorrow, it was her tears that eased their heartache. Mormon or Gentile, it mattered not to her. That you were in distress or grief was enough to call out the loving tenderness of this great heart, this "mother in Israel."

III.

ON THE MOUNTAIN SIDE.

Our village was so close under the Wasatch that on the longest summer days the sun rose little before seven o'clock. The upward slope began in the back yard, and our regular beat when looking for birds was up a steep lane leading to the mountain. When there were no birds on the stone walls to claim our attention, we stopped to admire the flowers along the lane, — small pink stars among the sage-brush, white stars shyly looking out from the high grass of neglected fence corners, bushy purple lupins and brilliant red "paint-brushes." Later in the year, wild roses and gorgeous masses of yellow flowers lightened up the lane. We looked at them with ignorant enjoyment, but when my friend's daughter came, she did them better justice, studying them with the appreciative eye of a botanist.

The sage-brush, with its delicate aromatic fragrance and varying tints, gave us almost as much pleasure as the flowers. It rarely approached the dullness of sage green, but varied from silvery white to the delicate shell pink of a sunset sky. Seen in great sheets over the lower slopes of the mountain, the sage was perhaps most effective; but its silvery sheen was particularly beautiful against the blue of the sky.

Climbing the lane we followed its joyous mountain brook, running with rapid music over the pebbles, or straying from its bed like a free thing of life to run over its green border, bending the long grass before it. Sometimes we plucked a nosegay of wild flowers and left it hidden under the bank to be freshened by the brook; and often, after our warm walk, would scoop up a handful of the clear cold water for a refreshing drink.

While my friend was listening to the " wandering voice " of the mysterious chat, or studying the secretive ways of a family of chewinks she had discovered in the sage-brush, I often climbed up beyond the end of the lane, where I could overlook the valley.

The feverish longing one has for the country in spring had possessed my blood before I left the city. The brick horizons and squares of sky had irritated my tired spirit. The lonely groups of trees, turning green on the outskirts, made me only more restless.

But now at last I was free. Alone on the mountain side, the sunshine of the broad heavens, the unbroken horizon, and the great sweep of the landscape lines were a deep rest and refreshment. Up beyond me the mountain swept gently toward the blue sky, its sunny slope darkened only by cloud shadows; the whole broad mountain side a solitude, its restful silence jarred by no footfall; its only suggestion of the figure of man a lone tree against the sky.

Looking up at the Wasatch, I was much impressed by its "range and sweep." From my position its clumps of oak-brush were mere cushions of green moss. High from above, a bird of prey came sailing down the mountain, projecting its shadow ahead. Now it would swoop close over a rocky ledge or sweep low over the side of cañon wall, — a mere seam to me, — then slowly sail across the face of the range, rising upward till it soared beyond the lofty crags at the summit. Above, below, farther, nearer, against the mountain, against the sky, it sailed and soared.

From the hillside as far as the eye could range, from the north around to the south, the view was a never-failing source of delight. It rested me to follow up and down the mountain with my eye — from the sky, down the broad slope over the spreading valley to the northern horizon, where low floating clouds melted into the blue.

Looking westward, a great mountain island rested on the still lake like some noble couchant animal. While all the distant ranges were blue or purple, this mountain ridge, Antelope Island, glowed warm in shades of brown, pink, or red. On some days the colors seen from the hillside were our chief pleasure. The lake became a rainbow, of blue, pink, buff, and vivid green bands, with the red island as a rich background.

But best of all our views was that to the southward. Day after day I climbed up to see it; without it our days seemed incomplete. Far beyond through the haze, rose serene, snow-covered mountains, white clouds resting motionless in the pale sky above them. Snow mountains were dimly reflected in the smooth blue lake at their feet; a boat with furled sail stood anchored by the sandy shore. Stilled by the calm of the lake and the strength of the hills, resting in the tenderness of the warm sunshine, with the blue sky arching over me, my spirit was filled with peace.

Seen from the level of the lake, the sides of the Wasatch are divided off into "benches," or terraces, that mark the former levels of Salt Lake — when it was "Lake Bonneville," an inland sea covering nearly twenty thousand square miles instead of two thousand. From the shore of the present shrunken lake you look back on the old beaches, the terraced mountain side covered with sheets of sage-brush. Above the last "high-water mark" you see clumps of dark oak-brush, and an outcrop of rugged cliff-like rock. Higher still you can distinguish the outlines of evergreen spires, where deer and even grizzly bears are found, and snow is said to lie in the gulches twenty feet deep all through the summer.

It was from the side of the first sage-brush bench that I used to overlook the lake and refresh myself with the breadth and sweep of the mountain outlines. When in listening mood, I could hear the meadow-lark's sweet song rising from the edge of the village; the chewink's cheerful voice and the lazuli bunting's merry round in the bushes about me; with the clamorous magpies' shouts as, like black arrows, they sped back and forth from the village.

From my eyrie I looked down on a house at the foot of the lane, belonging to the night watchman of a large Mormon city store, "Zion's Coöperative Mercantile Institution." It was one of the typical "rock" houses of the place, built of irregular blocks of stone plastered together. From my sunny hillside I took an indolent satisfaction in the life below. The watchman's son, a stripling in blue jeans, after doing a few "chores" with great deliberation, threw himself down in the orchard, and idly whipped the grass with a twig. When his sister, in a faded pink calico, drew the baby past him, he roused himself to whip at her dress, and at intervals, broken strains of a lazily whistled tune came up to me.

Below were signs of more animated life. A farmer was hard at work plowing. As the sun glanced from the steel, and the brown border grew on the square of green turf, I got delicious suggestions of fragrant earth and soft crumbling furrows. Below the village, smoke rose from a hurrying express train; but I was secure in the solitude of the mountain side; the brown lines of smoke soon vanished from my horizon, while the gleam from the plow shone in my thoughts.

A colt frisked about in a neighboring pasture, a black hen strolled leisurely up the lane, the magpies screamed, and a rock squirrel leaned inquiringly over a fence post. To my tired spirit they added the rest and peace of simple country life to the refreshment given by the sweeping lines of mountain and valley, and the great open sky, the broad free heavens over all.

As I rested on the warm ground among the fragrant sage-bushes, the glad voice of the mountain brook rang in my ears; cool and pure from the snow of the Wasatch, hurrying to fulfill its " priest-like task ; " rising at last into the sky to fall again free from stain in pure white snow upon the mountain tops. As I gazed dreamily into the blue sky, a beautiful butterfly, red against the sun, flew over my head straight on as if it would storm the mountain wall, — frail, airy flutterer, strong with the joy of climbing to heaven. I followed it with my eye — great radiant white clouds came puffing up over the mountains. My spirit rose exultant, catching inspiration from nature in its purity, strength, and radiant joy.

One morning, when wandering over the bench, I met three little maidens, one a bright, brown-eyed child, and one a gentle, blue-eyed little girl, looking for flowers in the sage-brush. When I admired their posies, they ran off eagerly to gather some for me, and brought them with the sweet childlike mixture of flutter and shyness. Their confidence was quickly gained, and they prattled gayly about the flowers. When I almost stepped on a cactus, they told me how some of the villagers cooked them. When we discovered some dodder, they told me how they used to coil the pretty orange-vine into birds' nests, and put it up in the trees, thinking the little birds would come and live in their nests. Before I left them they pointed out a big granite bowlder on the bench above us, exclaiming, "See? that is the frog rock: it looks like a frog;" and as I went down the mountain, my arms full of the bright flowers they had brought me, they ran merrily up to climb the rock. Looking from below I could distinguish three little forms, high up on the bowlder, and when I waved to them, they waved gayly back to me.

We often climbed the bench to watch the sunsets. They were so beautiful that we felt our loss if we missed a night from some point overlooking the lake.

On one of the rare occasions when the sky was overcast, the sun went down behind the gray curtain without a gleam; but soon, to our surprise, a line of red light ran along the edge of the curtain, and all that gray sky was made glad by the rich rose glow and its reflection in the lake beneath.

On another night, we had a sunset of wondrous color. The gold ball slid into the lake, leaving a sky of peaceful blue in which rested long golden bars. Then the gold caught fire, and the heavens were aflame with color and light. Above us, on the bench, a horn blew out in joyous exultant blasts. Gradually the rainbow colors faded, and the flaming cloud streamers melted away. At last there was left a sky of clear mauve, and out of its warm light the great evening star shone radiant above the lake. Other stars came out dimly overhead. The dark strong outline of the mountain slope cut the sky in a line of singular purity; crickets chirred around us; the peace of evening was upon us. A hush fell over all, and in the twilight calm the beautiful old hymn, "Nearer, my God, to Thee," came softly from the horn on the hillside. The peace of the fading sunset had come to the Mormon lad in the one beautiful yearning prayer in which Mormon and Gentile join with uplifted souls.

IV.

HORSEBACK RIDING.

My first inquiries on getting settled in Utah were for a horse and saddle. In looking for a saddle, I got a hint of the dark undercurrent of the outwardly peaceful village life. Going to the house of one of the white-haired patriarchs, I asked if he would rent me his saddle. He smiled in an embarrassed way, and mumbled, "The girl has got it," looking at the house across the street, where I had been told his second wife lived. I covered his confusion by a few remarks on the weather, and then said casually : —

"Could I see the saddle?"

"Yes," he answered hesitatingly, "you can go over."

He crossed the street with me, saying in a masterful way, "The girl is away, but I can show it to you." However, he rang the bell, and stood uneasily fumbling with the door waiting for an answer. As none came, he finally led me into the house. It was he who explained my errand to his wife, but she looked past him at me. I thought she would not meet his eye at all, but saw her at last look up at him; and that look gave me my first real understanding of polygamy. It was as if they were separated by an impassable black gulf of hatred. He lived across the street with his other wife; she and her children lived alone here.

In this case, however, I consoled myself by reflecting that it was the younger wife, not the old woman, who had the worst suffering. But at the next house where I looked for a saddle, — "the girl" having lent this one, — the old white-haired wife was living alone, her husband having gone to Canada with his young wife.

After getting a saddle, I looked about for a suitable horse. I was strongly attracted to one a man brought me to look at one day; but that night his sad-faced wife came in distress to the "mother in Israel" to warn her not to let me buy it; and the next morning the man himself came back to say he had decided not to sell, explaining, "If anything should happen, you'd blame me." Then I was advised of a horse advertised on the front of the post-office, — " One flea-bitten white horse to be sold by sheriff's sale from the estray pound;" but the stiff-kneed old wanderer passed on to the grocer's cart — for nine dollars.

After that, I was offered a horse for her feed, but her nerves were shattered and her bones were bare; and after she had almost upset the buggy before our own door, she went back to her pasture.

At last, the son of a Mormon elder brought me a handsome chestnut horse. His mane was roached, zebra fashion, and he had a conspicuous brand on his hip; but I consoled myself by his flavor of "local color;" and before the season was over, prided myself on the distinguished air conferred by his pompadour mane; and rode by the court-house with a feeling of proprietorship, remembering complacently that his brand was recorded in its books.

Experience had taught me that it was cheaper to buy a horse than to rent one, but in this case the " hard times " affected my speculation, obliging me to sell for fifteen dollars in September, when I had paid thirty in June.

The honest Mormon lad concluded our bargain with a bill of sale, which he and the village merchant drew up after long consultation behind the desk of the store, while I inspected ginghams. It announced that I had bought " one brown horse, branded £ on left hip, with one white foot."

I was surprised and pleased by the boy's affection for the horse, though when I asked the animal's name, he acknowledged gruffly that he "didn't call him anything but Jumbo." He told me, if he got frightened, to " speak *kindly* to him ; " if he would not go, to " whip him a *little*." And when I had taken the lad's bill of sale, he looked so downcast, I felt reproached.

I suspected that he dreaded telling his old mother of the sale, for I had heard that she "raised Jumbo from a colt, and thought everything of him." To mend matters I said, "Tell your mother I'll take good care of Jumbo, and when I leave Utah, I'll give you the first chance to buy him back." His face brightened with surprise, and he exclaimed earnestly, "I'd like to buy him back if I could get the money."

To assure the old mother that her pet was not ill used, I rode him down to see her. She lived on a lonely farm, half way to the lake; her little house, overshadowed by its big haystacks, standing alone in the midst of the meadows. The elder had been gathered to the saints, and his two widows mourned his loss, — one in the city, the other out on the farm. My friend's strong old face softened when Jumbo put his nose up against her, and her steady gray eyes filled with tears. She said apologetically, " He was such a pet: Nellie used to ride him bareback, and he'd follow us all around the yard. I was tellin' them last night I 'd rather you 'd take him away and I 'd never see him again, than to think he might be sold to some one who would use him bad." She told me with pride how, when he had been taken to Idaho, he had gotten away and come back home two hundred miles: " When I got home from Mrs. Talcott's, down to the switch, there he stood at the gate."

I became strongly attached to the upright old Mormon woman. I had already learned what sterling virtue is to be found among the Mormon sisters; but my prejudices were still further broken down by the almost Puritan character of the elder's widow. She had borrowed a small sum to repair her house, and now, in the hard times, was living alone with her son — she confessed her loneliness to me — to let her daughter work in the village. Meanwhile, day after day she stood in her stocking feet in the hot sun, picking currants to sell for her debt. She said, "I can't bear to be owin' anything; it worries me most to death."

She told me what good men her husband's people were. After his death, she had gone to visit them. "They all made a great deal of me, they thought so much of my husband," she said in a tone of reverence for one so great among his kin; adding simply, unconscious of the pathos of her words, "I did n't know exactly what to do. I was n't used to being made so much of." Then, reflectively, "When I came home, I told my son what good men his father's folks was, and told him he ought never to do anything to disgrace his name."

With a certain dignified reserve about her own affairs, she took a friendly interest in her neighbors. When she found that I was in Utah without my family, her motherly old heart warmed to me. She urged me to come in and sit with her. She said, "It seems as if you 'd be lonesome away from your folks, so;" adding sympathetically, as she stood in the sun beside Jumbo, "It seems so as if we ought to help each other, in this world."

Her kindly heart was still troubling her for what she considered a neglected duty of thirty years back. She had just moved to her little two-room house, when her husband, the pioneer elder, brought home "a poor English gentleman," an invalid traveling alone, whom the elder had found just after he had been robbed of all he had. The good people took in the stranger, and cared for him solicitously till he felt able to go on to find his friends. But when he wrote back to them he said that he had not been able to find them, — the country and people were in such an unsettled state, — and from that time on they never heard from him. In their uneventful life, year after year they looked for word, but as none ever came they thought he must have died, and they reproached themselves sadly for having let him go. "We might have kept him a few months, anyway, if we did n't have much room;" the good old woman said. "It seems as if we had not done right by him. I never could forgive myself;" and her kindly old face was full of distress — after thirty years.

Sometimes when Jumbo and I stopped at the little house, the daughter was at home helping the mother dry her corn, or doing some work too hard for the old woman to do alone. " Ma ain't very strong now," the girl would say sadly. While I sat in the saddle the two would leave their work to chat with me, picking clover for Jumbo, and bringing me out ice-cold buttermilk fresh from the churning.

The daughter, a bright responsive girl of twenty, was to go to the village school in the winter. Her mother confided to me, " She takes to books, and I want to have her have a good schoolin'; none of the rest of the children took to books. The only trouble with her is her arithmetic; she says that's so hard for her she's most a mind to give up goin'. She's a great hand to read." When I asked the girl what she liked to read she said brightly, " Oh, most anything;" but added patiently, " I've never seen any books except at school and at the store; they have some paper-covered books at the store, sometimes."

She liked to make rag carpets, she told me, because it took up the time! I was appalled. All that I had known of the meagreness and wasted energy of farm and village life came back to me with fresh force, — I had forgotten it was so bad. I remembered what the girl's poor old mother had confided to me about "getting so lonesome and worn out thinking," on her isolated farm, that sometimes it seemed as if she could n't stand it. And I recalled with a shudder the statistics I had known about the number of farmers' wives who go insane. Then I thought of the daughters, and it seemed a short step from the wives who go insane to the daughters whose eager minds are ready to respond to any interest offered them, whose energy is waiting to be used in any earnest work that calls — sitting down to make rag carpets to pass the time!

I wanted to start out on a village crusade, to put to use the young strong life of our countrywomen, so full of the common sense and simple goodness that our civilization is in need of, and, in turn, to save them from stagnation, from the bare dreary lives whose drudgery ends with the asylum. It seemed such an easy matter to bring farm and village life into touch with the centres of intelligence, in this age of circulating libraries, Channing Auxiliaries, Home Culture Clubs, Chautauqua Circles, and Boston Home Study Societies, together with the thousand other forms of the university extension movement.

The Mormons themselves have an organization,— a young people's society,— but while its work includes an elementary review of natural history, the object of the society is to teach the young people the church doctrines.

In the case of my friend, as doubtless in many cases, much was within her reach, but she did not know how to get at it. I went to the best Salt Lake library for her, and the librarian gladly consented to let the girl draw books; her brother could get them for her when he took in loads of hay. And when I left Utah she was studying over Chautauqua circulars trying to decide about taking work in that society.

The poor child had so few pleasures, I was sorry to be depriving her of her occasional "bareback" rides on Jumbo. The old fellow still kept his interest in the family and responsibility for their affairs, and gave me a good laugh one day on the way to their house. Grazing loose in the lane we found a mare and colt which Jumbo recognized as belonging to the family. He was greatly disturbed to find them so far from home, and, walking up to them, tried to round them up and drive them back. I could hardly persuade him to neglect the duty.

In our barn-yard, Jumbo had the same sense of responsibility. When our colt's mother was away, he drove the little fellow down to water before him, as if he had full charge of its bringing up. The little creature became so fond of him it would follow him around the yard most affectionately. Indeed, Jumbo became a favorite with all the family. The children picked green apples for him, and rode him bareback about the yard; the boarders shook the mulberry-trees to give him fresh supplies of berries; and even the "transient" drummer stroked the old fellow's neck in passing through the yard.

We had long happy mornings together, Jumbo and I; wading through the pebbly brooks — it was a marvel he did not drink them dry — and rambling along, enjoying the fresh air and sunshine, the mountains and the meadows.

One ride I liked better than he, — through the sage-brush to a picturesque old flour-mill surrounded by oak-brush, in the mouth of a cañon. The rush of the water, the big mill-stones lying outside the mill, frightened him so that the miller, sitting in his cottage doorway, laid down his newspaper to be ready to come to my aid. Business was so dull with the miller, I felt glad when I met a boy on horseback going for a sack of flour.

Up the cañon, this side of the divide, we were told there was a waterfall thirty feet high; so one morning we went to look for it. We followed along the swift stream where the water-ousels live, till the cañon walls came close and our horses had to pick their way over the narrow trail, — a solid mass of loose stone brought down the cañon by the spring freshets, — overgrown with stiff bushes that threatened to brush us off our saddles.

We forded the swift stream back and forth, getting well splashed when the horses plunged deep between the rolling rocks. Though Jumbo carried me bravely, he did not share my enthusiasm: the climb up the trail was too steep for his portly form. When we took breath in the shade, we would drink from the ice-cold springs that bubbled up among moss and ferns to run down in white cascades over the rocks.

At last we came to a place where the trail seemed to end. Hidden under the brush we espied an old lumber wagon-wheel rusted with age, and in it my friend discovered stores that made us think of the village gold mine. By looking closely we found hints of a trail leading off mysteriously through the bushes, straight up the cañon wall. From the village a dark spot had been pointed out to us, high on the mountain, as the mouth of this mine; and the reticent prospectors who had been going and coming during the summer had invested the old claim with an air of romance. Once I had seen a miner driving his loaded pack-mule through the village toward the mountain, and later had been surprised to see it coming home alone, bared of its burdens; when the people explained that a few villagers were still trying to work out the gold, some hinting that great riches were hidden there.

We were so much interested in tracking out the source of all this mystery, we felt quite as if we had followed the rainbow to the pot of gold; and for the moment overlooked our disappointment in having to turn home without finding the waterfall. As we came down the trail we got beautiful pictures of the blue lake, set in the V frame of the cañon walls.

Another day, when climbing the bench,

my friend got off to look for the road that vanished in sage-brush, and came face to face with a rattlesnake, — one of the two I saw in Utah.

The long summer evenings were especially pleasant for riding. The sun, slanting across the lake, vivified the green meadows and oak-brush; and after it went down in the lake, a warm glow spread over the sides of the Wasatch. One evening we stayed out till the great round moon came up over the mountains, when, with the cool breeze in our faces, we rode home, casting our galloping shadows behind us.

But my favorite ride was across the meadows to the lake. After living under the shadow of the mountains, it was a rest to wander about in the great sunny meadows.

In May, when the wild-flowers were in bloom on the mountain sides, some of the fields were a mass of blue flowers; and a little later, the dark marsh grass was lit up by patches of yellow wild-flowers. Then came the clover, — purple, instead of pink, but as fragrant as our own Eastern clover. And when the air was sweet with this lucern, the gleaming yellow mustard blossomed along the way; not the common low mustard of the East, but the high mustard trees of the West, so graphically described by Helen Hunt in " Ramona." Along the roads, it grew above Jumbo's head, and whole fields were yellow with it, reflecting back the sunshine of the sky. The mustard, too, had a delicious perfume, almost that of heliotrope.

When the purple fields of lucern had been mowed and the exquisitely tinted grasses of the marshy meadows were cut, the warm summer air quivered over the straw-colored fields, and the delicate blue sky seemed to rest tenderly above the glistening stubble. Then I met great loads of hay being driven in from the meadows, not to barns, — for Utah has little need of such shelters, — but to the great golden haystacks that stand out against the blue skies there. Some of the roads were bordered with rosy hedges of pink weeds, each one standing like a huge candelabrum with pink lights, — *cleomes*, my botanical friend called them.

Then came the August flowers, the pink wild roses brightening the roads, the wild sunflowers growing by the dark marshes and bordering the meadow fences, as our goldenrod does at home. The fields fairly smiled with the sunflowers, the long rows of them turning on their stalks to raise their bright faces to the sun.

The meadow road was so little frequented that the birds of the neighborhood gathered on its fences, flying up as Jumbo cantered by. We often scared up noisy flocks of blackbirds from the cat-tails, the old birds anxiously bustling their young out of the way. Once we passed close to a big baby dove, trying to balance himself on the top wire of the fence, and bewildered him greatly, for his mother had evidently told him to stay right there till she came back. At one point in the road, for some days, we were met by patrolling killdeer, who escorted us safely past the hiding-places of their young.

There were pleasant surprises along the way now and then. One day I startled a small brown heron standing in the road, making him strike such an attitude that I wanted to laugh in his face. He raised his long neck, fixing his gaze upon the zenith, like an abstracted philosopher rather than the reed he would have me take him for. As we bore down on him, he sprang suddenly into the air, but as suddenly dropped down among the protecting cat-tails. Near the same place I saw a great blue heron rise slowly from a swale and follow the curving stream, pursued by a corps of blackbirds, till he went down among the rushes.

A sage-hen once whirred across the road ahead of us. And when an irrigation ditch made a temporary lake in the middle of the road, a ladylike wader "went to sea in a bowl."

When the grasshoppers threatened to become a "plague" again, — though Brigham Young could no longer bring the gulls by his prayers, as the Mormons told us he had done before, — the birds came up from the lake to feed on them, and I often passed white cohorts sitting in the meadows.

Jumbo did his best to prevent the grasshoppers eating up the crops, by eating them up himself. He would have grazed the roadsides bare if I had not reasoned with him.

He and I had two friends on the meadow road,— a great motherly sorrel mare and her big colt. They seemed lonely, pastured by themselves out in the great meadows, and stood close by the roadway fence, as if for the chance of company. Jumbo used to walk up and put his nose over the gate to them. First the mother stepped up quickly, to protect her colt; but she soon came to know us, and I flattered myself that she missed our friendly calls when we no longer passed her way.

The meadows were not without the spicy flavor of wild life. When Jumbo was eating lucern one day, I discovered a pretty little cotton-tail rabbit only a few yards from us. He crouched close, and his sides beat as Jumbo grazed nearer; but he let the old fellow come almost up to him before he bounded off to his burrow. It was pleasant to think that the pretty creature had his home so close to our path.

A still stronger flavor of the wild life of the bottoms came to us one evening on our way to the lake. For a long time we drove toward the sunset, a radiant sky over us; but as we neared the lake, twilight settled down. Suddenly from the dusk of the roadside pasture a small herd of cattle came running toward us. Straining our eyes in the gloom, we recognized the gaunt forms of two hungry wolves. We pulled up our horses, and saw that the cattle had put their calves in the middle of their herd, — as buffaloes do when in danger, — for the wolves were in pursuit of the calves. Defeated by our unexpected arrival, the lank beasts slunk away, and we traced their course by a flock of blackbirds that flew after them in tumultuous excitement, disappearing in the darkness.

But though the meadows were so full of interest, with their flowers, their birds, and their beasts, I could not stay to enjoy them always. In August my rides came to an end. I was going away, and, alas! could not take Jumbo with me.

Before leaving, I rode down to give the Mormon boy the promised chance to buy back his horse. He was mowing, but drew up his team to talk with me. "Times are so hard I can't sell my hay," he said. "And horses are so cheap now. I can get anything I want up to Salt Lake for from five to fifteen dollars" — which I knew to be a fact. I offered him "time," but, like his mother, he did not choose to be in debt. "I want him if I can get the money," he said finally, promising to let me know. During our conversation Jumbo had stepped up and put out his nose to the lad, and I suspect that settled the matter, for his master was a silent boy on a lonely farm. At any rate, the money was found, and Jumbo went back to his old home. Then the reserved boy confessed to a friend that he had felt "lost" without Jumbo; that the old fellow used to follow him everywhere, would run behind all the way to Salt Lake when he was driving in hay and he did n't know how to get along without him. "It's the last time he'll ever be sold to anybody as long as I can keep him," he had declared.

He showed his pride in his old companion by immediately roaching the mane I had let grow to unseemly pompadour length. He rode him up on an errand before I left. We were all standing by the gate when he came, and a delighted cry of "Jumbo!" burst out as he turned the corner. The old fellow put his nose against me so affectionately it nearly destroyed the stoicism I had mustered to send him away; and when he tried to go into the barn-yard, the whole family shouted approval. But at my last glimpse of him, Jumbo had been up on the mountain with his master, and the light of his old life was in his eyes — he had gone home and gone back to his allegiance. It gave me a passing pang, but I was glad to remember that I had returned him to his family; and it was a real pleasure to know that the poor girl whom I had been depriving of her rides was enjoying her pet once more.

V.

THE LITTLE HOME UNDER THE BENCH.

ONE evening when we were watching the sunset from the rocks on the bench, two little girls came running up the lane. When almost up to us, they turned and fled laughing at their own daring. We called after them, and they ventured a little nearer. Loitering about the sage-brush, trying to get courage to come to us, they discovered a rare plant, and in the dusk held out its beautiful white flower to us. My friend hurried to them for it, and their shyness vanished — the white flower made us friends. Soon they were sitting on the rocks prattling freely to us, the little sister snuggled under my arm. They were Swedes, they told us, adding confidences about their kittens; while the little brother, who had wandered up the lane to join our group, regaled us with bits of spicy boy wisdom.

When we started home, they urged us to stop at their house; they would show us all their kittens. They led us stumbling along in the dark, through their gate, beside a long grapevine trellis almost as high as their little house, to the light that shone out through the glass in the small front door. The children called to their mother, and a fair-haired Scandinavian woman came out. She was a little abashed by the sudden downfall of strange "ladies," but greeted us cordially in her pretty foreign English.

At the sound of voices a flaxen-haired baby girl sat up in the middle of the big bed that filled the corner, and opened her great blue eyes wonderingly. When we tried to make friends, the little darling began to cry, so her mother took her in her arms and held her close, caressing her while she talked to us.

She apologized for the children's beds, made of quilts laid on chairs; the two big beds and the sideboard, holding the best china, filled the room. Her husband was a skilled shoemaker, she told us, but as there were already three of his trade in the village, he had gone away to find work, and they were just waiting to be sent for. The children were lonely without their father, she said, and we saw that her heart was sad.

While she talked to us with baby Cecilia in her arms, the little people ran out and brought in their kittens. They put them down in our laps, dropping on their knees at our feet to stroke the pretty creatures.

When we left, their mother courtesied as she timidly shook hands, thanking "the ladies" for coming; while the children clung around us, asking eagerly if we would be on the mountain the next night. It was a homely scene, but the sweet family life warmed our hearts; we felt that we had indeed found a home "where love dwelt."

A few evenings later, as I climbed the lane, little Hilda, in a bright red frock, came running down to meet me. Not far behind, leading baby Cecilia, came her mother, looking very picturesque and foreign in a bright blue gown and white apron, with a white kerchief tied over her head. She was too tired to climb the bench, so I spread out my shawl beside the road in front of her cottage, and we sat down to watch the sunset there.

As we looked down beyond the village at the lake, she told me about her old home on the coast of Sweden; where, as a girl, she used to climb out on a branch of a great tree in her garden, to watch the sunset through the rigging of the ships. "There," she said, "I could see, oh so much water and ships!"

When I took off my hat she said that when she was a girl she liked to go about without a hat; that she loved to go out on the hills to look at the flowers and watch the sunsets and clouds and stars and sky; that she was perfectly happy all alone, wanting no companion if she could only be there.

She told of her mother's beautiful garden in Sweden, and how, as a child, she had had a little bed of wild-flowers in it. Now she was longing for a cottage of her own, where she could plant flowers and make a real home for herself, "when my husband finds a place."

While we were talking, the children brought out their kittens, and the frolicsome little creatures scampered madly about, climbing the picket fence and making excited sallies up the sides of the trees.

The children played around us with the same abandon. "Benjamin," as his mother called him, helped the neighbor's children make a haycock of sage-brush, and then, with boyish glee, gave it a kick that scattered it down the hillside. Hilda, the little red bird, ran racing down the steep lane again and again for pure fun.

When Clara, the older sister, came in from doing her neighbor's milking, she brought her doll, and dressed it up for me to see; while Hilda snuggled under my arm, and the blue-eyed baby Cecilia, no longer afraid, brought me sprays of sage, one at a time. Once, at her mother's bidding, according to the pretty Scandinavian custom, the baby lisped, " Thank you " when I took a spray from her; but she liked best to have me thank her, and laughed gleefully to hear me.

Then the children brought out their family albums, to show me their father; the mother telling me proudly how handsome he looked in his uniform when he was serving his term in the army. " He play on the accordion and the fiddle," she said; but added sadly, " When he went away, he took the music with him." She had no heart to go up on the bench alone now. " Sometimes the children will sit down in the house, and cry for him," she said; adding, " They were all happy when he was here." " Oh, he is a fine man, a fine man!" she exclaimed, with the pride of a wife in her eyes. And the children eagerly showed me picture cards they had just received, on which their father had written messages in Swedish, asking them to think of him on his birthday.

While they played around us, their mother told me of the little ones she had lost. "Such *pooty* little girls," she moaned; crying out, "Oh, if you could have *seen* the children," with a look in her eyes that made my heart ache. "It took me quite a bit when the last one went," she said sadly; going on to tell me how her little one died in the night, and when the neighbors came to her at sunset the next day, she did not know that breakfast-time had passed. Baby Cecilia, meantime, had crept into her mother's lap, and now crooned in her arms, petted her face and drew it down to kiss in a way that took the sadness out of the mother's eyes, and made her press her baby tenderly to her breast.

When the sun had set and I got up to go home, the children jumped up to follow me, calling eagerly, "You come too, ma; you come too." When we said good-night, they clamored that we should go up on the mountain the next night, still including their mother in their sweet, earnest way, "and you will come too, ma." Their mother gave a quaint courtesy when I shook hands with her, hoping I'd excuse her, if the children troubled us, for she couldn't keep them from running after us — poor lonely little creatures.

One evening when out on horseback I rode up to the little house under the bench to show Jumbo to the children. They fairly danced around him, all exclaiming over him at once; except baby Cecilia, who clasped her hands in silent delight over the "pretty horsie." She did not quite dare touch him till her mamma took her inside the fence and lifted her up behind the protecting pickets; when she leaned over, stretching out her baby hand timidly to pat his soft neck. It was a pretty sight.

The old fellow evidently liked my little family. He put his nose up against the fence and stood motionless, as if afraid to stir lest he should frighten them, all the while looking down on them with interested friendly eyes. We were all enjoying each other so much I was sorry to ride on, though the bright sunset clouds were fading over the mountains above us, and below the bench the sun was setting in golden light over the lake.

We usually watched the sunset from the rocks on the hillside, and it came to be understood that the children would join us there.

On the 10th of August, the great meteor night, the mother and all the children climbed the bench with us. We passed the shed where Clara did her milking, "the cow that kicked" having its leg safely tied up to the wall; while the owner of the cows, a strong-faced old woman too rheumatic to milk, sat on a stool in a dark doorway, where she could look in and watch the child, or look out, down upon the village life.

We climbed through the sage-brush, taking our station in the midst of it on a huge bowlder, warm with stored sunshine. Baby Cecilia amused herself sliding down its smooth face, stretching up her little arms to have me draw her up again. She sat in my lap quite contentedly for a little while, and picked out the bright evening star, pointing it out to me with her baby finger. But when one of her mother's sad Swedish songs rang out from the starlit stillness of the mountain side, the baby stretched out her little hands to her mamma.

The mother rocked the little one in her arms, crooning a soft lullaby; and soon the baby's pink sunbonnet nodded forward, the plump arms rested motionless side by side, the dimpled hands lay fast asleep. Such wonderful little hands! When I touched them and they closed around my fingers, I held them tenderly and reverently. At such moments motherhood seems the most beautiful thing that life can hold.

While we were waiting for the meteors, we pointed out the constellations to the children, and Ben went on to discover one for himself. "A pistol!" he exclaimed, tracing it out for me with enthusiasm. Clara became greatly interested in astronomical matters, but was inclined to doubt there being no "up" or "down" to the sky.

For some time we saw only small meteors, and Ben at last remarked in a tone of dissatisfaction, "The big stars don't seem to shoot." As it grew darker, however, the meteors came thick and fast, little and big, till the children shouted excitedly whenever one shot through the sky. After watching quietly for a time, their mother said meditatively, " It seems so funny — up in the sky — it seems as if somebody took a light and run." When we reluctantly left our rock the mother had to carry the sleeping baby in her arms, Ben proudly piloting us home through the sage-brush.

When we were getting ready to leave the village in the fall, my friend took up her hammock, hanging it under the orchard trees for the children; and it was a pretty sight to see Ben swinging his little sisters under the apple-trees, Hilda putting her arm protectingly around baby Cecilia.

We were glad to know before leaving the little family that good news had come from their father. He had found work and was coming soon to take them to their new home. So when we waved our final good-by to them in their garden, the mother surrounded by her loving little ones, underneath our sadness was the feeling that their loneliness was nearly over, their music was coming back to them.

VI.

VILLAGE LIFE.

From my rocking-chair under the trees of our yard I looked out upon the village street with interest and curiosity; for the sights and sounds of a village street in Utah differ widely from those of a New York or New England town.

The sound of galloping hoofs was as common as that of wheels. Men passed in saddles, and boys bareback, — two on a horse, — doing errands and driving home the cows, or running races, tearing madly up the streets. Even the little boys whose feet reached only half way down the horses' sides seemed as much at home on an unruly pony as on a seesaw. For almost every one raises horses in Utah. Nearly every wagon that passed was followed by one or more colts.

But more striking than the horseback riders were the frequently passing emigrant wagons. The whole family were often seen looking out from under the white wagon cover; while the team was flanked by colts. The people usually looked tired and disheveled, huddled in with their household gods; but I remember one bright picture: on the seat between the young father and mother, a pretty baby boy with long yellow curls was hugging the family tabby cat under his arm. In one lumber wagon that passed, the family sat on the front seat while two calves stood up behind.

Sometimes in riding through the village toward dusk, I would pass an emigrant wagon drawn up in a shady spot; the horses resting unharnessed and the family eating their supper on the grass under the village trees.

Herds of cattle and flocks of sheep often passed by, driven by tired-looking men on horseback. When the sheep were going to a winter "range," they were followed by a tent on wheels, — a huge emigrant " sheep wagon," with a stovepipe projecting from the top of the roof.

On Decoration Day, the whole town passed by our yard. There were no soldiers buried in the village, but the people observed the day by decorating the graves of their own dead. When on the mountain side in the morning, I found men as well as children gathering flowers in the sage-brush. In our family, our sweet-faced schoolteacher arranged flowers for the grave of the old grandfather who had recently died; and the little grandchildren filed out of our gate with their arms full of flowers, taking them first across the street to the desolate old grandmother, and then carrying them on to the village cemetery to lay reverently upon the newly made mound.

Almost all the villagers went out to the graveyard, though it was a long walk in the hot sun. Mothers passed, wheeling their baby carriages; men, women, and children went by with their arms full of blossoms; while some walked past carrying great clothes-baskets full of flowers.

There was no service, we were told; but "the band played and the people laid their flowers on their graves;" and when it was over, some good women went around putting flowers on the neglected mounds "that every grave should have some flowers that day." Our informant added to her neighbor, "They talk about Susan not caring for Joe! She just shook. I guess she thought a sight more of him than some that says more."

Not long after this, the village had another event to talk over — this time of a less saddening nature. It was the "Old People's Party." It seems that the Mormons have adopted the interesting custom of giving an annual "party" to all the old people of Utah. This year it was at Ogden, and there were said to be twelve hundred there over seventy years of age. The old people wore badges of different colors according to their ages, — seventy, eighty, or ninety. The governor and many of the principal citizens were present, speeches were made, prizes given to the oldest, and refreshments served to the old people by the young people. A number went from our village.

But as a rule our neighbors did not travel much. Outside life touched ours mainly in passing. Most of the varieties of travelers affecting village life stopped for a meal or a night's lodging with our good landlady.

Once, when we went over to dinner we found an emigrant wagon under the trees in our yard, and a tired-looking woman brought her baby in to dinner. At another time the stranger was a sheep-herder from the desolate sheep ranges of Idaho. One night our curiosity was excited by two men who came to the door while we were at supper, to ask if they could get a meal. Before sitting down to table, one of them — a huge fellow — took off his cow-boy hat and laid a six-shooter and cartridge belt on the bench. When asked if he were hunting, he hesitated, and then smiling significantly at his companion said, "Yes, we are hunting." Whether they were prospectors or sheriffs they did not say, and no one seemed to care to inquire.

But most of our " transients " were mild traveling men on their way through the Territory. Drummers brought their trunks to the house, spreading their goods on beds, tables, and chairs for the inspection of the village shop-keepers, who came in their shirt sleeves to look over the stock. Dentists came out from Salt Lake, and all the town flocked to have its aching teeth pulled.

Once we got a hint of a romance. A sheepish-looking boy and girl stopped till the court-house should be open; and though observers of the hammock under the trees gathered signs of hesitation from tears on her part and excited talk on his, when the hour came they were off to the court-house, got a license, and were married — poor foolish children.

The mother in Israel told us of a similar romance she had tried to prevent. In that case the young girl had run away from home with a man the good mother knew to be an evil character. So she had taken the poor child to her heart and had done her best to persuade her to go home before it was too late; but with no success. She was married: her old father died from the shock; and her husband was finally shot as a horse-thief.

Traveling men from the South told us exciting bits of war history; but more of our visitors discussed living history; the silver question was the excitement of the summer. When the morning paper came, the first question asked by men and women was, "What is the price of silver to-day?" One old prospector, with mild blue eyes and a long beard, grew indignant as he talked about it. "The people in the East will wish they had silver yet," he exclaimed wrathfully, adding with fervor, "The Comstock Lode supplied the sinews of war in the Rebellion;" and "anything that government has a mind to put its stamp on will carry."

Another prospector, who came to examine the old gold mine in the mountain above the village, told us of the excitement of an Antelope Island ranchman. Years before, "a college man" had told him that the Salt

Lake held a quarter of one per cent of gold in solution. After long pondering, the ranchman at last invented a process for extracting the gold. By his premise there were forty-five billions of gold in the lake, which it would cost only five billions to extract; leaving forty billions for circulation — more gold than there was in the world. Eureka! He went to the city with his story, and some business men telegraphed President Cleveland his solution of the silver problem; nothing remained to be done but to demonetize gold and remonetize silver — for gold would soon be far too abundant!

But all these discussions were like the whistle of the express train passing us on its way from New York to San Francisco, — a mere echo of the outside life of the world. Our swiftest currents ran through beds of brooks — still a long distance from the sea.

I had a striking illustration of this one day when at the post-office. The door of the private office was cautiously unlocked and the head of the assistant appeared, mysteriously beckoning me in. When the door had closed carefully upon us a qualm of trepidation passed over me. What had I to do in this securely guarded inner apartment? The assistant spoke no word, but stood back in humility, leaving the weighty matter to be broached by the superior officer alone. Even he hesitated a moment. Then he came forward, and said gravely, "The 'overdue stamp' on your package was not canceled last night before you took it away. It is your privilege and *right*" — with the emphasis of one who has decided a vital ethical problem — " it is your privilege and *right* to see it canceled." Whereupon, with a solemn official flourish, he raised the black punch in the air and brought it down, canceling the two cent-stamp! I stammered, "Oh! — yes — thank you," and beat a hasty retreat.

Our village bore the title of "city," but in our lanes downy yellow ducklings waddled up the banks of the puddles through stems of ballooning dandelions; humming-birds darted about the white tops of the blossoming locust-trees on the main streets, and I let my horse drink from pools in the mountain brooks along the chief highways.

In going to and fro between the great beautiful blue lake and the mountain side where we watched the sunsets, I passed a small brick building that looked like a storehouse. I was startled when told that it was a jail, but then thought it merely a useless piece of local machinery. But after I had been resting in the peaceful village life most of the summer, I heard with horror that all those months a young boy and a hardened burglar had been shut up there together, awaiting trial.

It was a rude shock to find that while I had been wandering at will, enjoying the beautiful country life, in the heart of this haven of rest there were fellow-beings shut off from it all, living under the worst conditions of city life.

It was the first time I had been brought face to face with the evils of our county jail system, and I came up against a case of typical horrors.

For nearly six months the young boy

and the hardened criminal were confined together, awaiting trial. During that time a boy and a young man served out a three weeks' term for chicken stealing. And I was told that an escaped murderer, whom the sheriff had rearrested in the neighborhood, was put in with them until he could be taken back to the penitentiary. What more typical "school of crime" could one have? Nothing was lacking but the innocent witness who is often locked in our county jails to make sure of his testimony in a case of distant trial.

As the prisoners were county prisoners, the "city" had no right to give them work, so all through those months the two had been confined in idleness: the old criminal with nothing to do but plan future crime; the young boy, whom the village pitied as "a pretty boy," with nothing to do but to learn what the older man had to teach. The sheriff, who was a very kind-hearted man, did what he could for them. To give them work, he took a wagon to pieces and carried it to jail for one of the chicken thieves, a painter, to paint. And although he was under such heavy bonds that an escape would have ruined him, the good man several times took the band to the hayfield with him. But with such exceptions, the two were confined for nearly six months without work or exercise.

The mother of the "pretty boy" wrote pitiful letters to the sheriff from her distant home, asking how it was that her child had ever fallen into such disgrace.

But though there was a vague feeling of sympathy in the town, and a few families sent paper-covered novels to the jail, month after month passed, and no mother in all that village went near the boy to try to counteract the effect of the burglar's influence, to try to do for that anguished mother's boy what they would have her do for theirs, — no mother in all that village but our great-hearted landlady, who, here as ever, proved a "mother in Israel." She not only went to the jail, but won the boy's confidence so that he told her about his mother, giving her his home address that she might write and give the poor woman news of him.

She came away from the jail with her motherly heart aching. It seemed so easy for the boy to be made a good man.

I went with her to the jail once or twice. The boy and the two chicken thieves came to the barred door and talked to us, looking up at us frankly, with faces that showed only a trace of hardness; and when they became interested in the games we were teaching them, they might have been taken for any village boys. But in the back of the room, the colorless-faced burglar paced up and down like a caged animal. The boys shrank as he came near them, and our hearts sank as we thought indignantly of the effect months of such association would have on this young boy, whose mother was sending him the "Youth's Companion."

We tried to collect some games and wholesome reading matter for the boys, and we felt that if anything could keep their belief in goodness it would be the influence of the good mother's visits.

But at best, we were working against a vast system whose machinery seemed fitted to turn out men only better trained in the ways of crime. Public intelligence, public thoughtfulness, seemed the only hope; public thoughtlessness, as great a crime as any committed by men inside the prison walls.

VII.

FLASH LIGHTS.

We had become so engrossed in the peaceful side of village life — what with our chickens and cows, and our views of mountain and lake — that we had almost forgotten where we were. One day, however, something was said about polygamy, when some one quietly remarked that our cook was one of the former bishop's *sixty-three* children, and that her mother was one of his *seven* wives. We awoke with a start, remembering with a sense of shock that we were in Utah.

Not long after, the mother wanted some peaches from the bishop's orchard, and I volunteered to go for them on horseback, secretly glad of an excuse to get sight of this marvelous family.

When near the place I inquired discreetly not for the bishop's house, but for the house where Mary's mother lived. But it is hard for the youthful mind to classify sixty-three children — even if they be his own half brothers. And although children fairly swarmed about the door-steps and in the yards, at each inquiry they told me that "Mary's mother" lived in "the next house."

When I finally found her, I did my errand, and then sat in the saddle pondering the situation. Here were three houses — an adobe, a rock house, and a brick one — that made three. Across the street were two more — five; up the road, another — six. The seventh wife [the first] was dead; she had gone insane and died when the second wife was taken. I drew a long breath before I could realize the situation. I caught sight of a gray beard in the shrubbery, but did not really see the patriarch that day.

One morning we breakfasted with a man of so much more intelligence than the ordinary "transient," that I inquired his name and business. "He is a whitewasher, and has come to do the kitchen," the mother told me; concluding: "He has just come back from a mission to England"! After that I often saw him on a Sunday, in a black broadcloth suit, returning from the Mormon "meeting-house."

We were continually having surprises of this kind to remind us where we were. When I bought a bottle of ammonia, I read with a start the mystic letters on the label, "Z. C. M. I."—Zion's Coöperative Mercantile Institution. Over the door of one of the principal stores in town this was shortened to "COÖP," and every one spoke familiarly of "the Coöp." The building next door to the Coöp bore the mysterious sign of "Bishop's Store House;" it proved to be the village tithing house.

The domestic tragedies I stumbled on in looking for a saddle were saddening enough, but one day we got a sharper flash of light upon polygamy. My friend and I were wandering about the village looking for nests to watch, and were led by the song of a grosbeak down a byway to a farm-yard gate. As it looked peaceful and quiet, we let ourselves in. The cows were lying in the shade chewing their cud, "red-wings" were feeding their young in a flowering bit of marsh at the head of the broad sunny meadows, where the bobolinks' voices rang merrily.

Our grosbeak was singing among the fragrant blossoms of a great locust that shaded the big rambling farmhouse. Through an open door I looked into the neat little kitchen, its window bright with house-plants, and saw a slender young girl swaying back and forth over the ironing board — I could almost smell the warm iron on the fresh linen. When I went to ask for a drink she was no disappointment — with her big blue eyes, fair hair, rosy cheeks, and a fresh happy face it did you good to look at. She took a glass and went out to fill it at an ice-cold bubbling spring.

When we spoke of the big locusts, she

said that her mother had lived there thirty years and would not have one of the trees cut down. She had had large offers for the place last winter, but would not sell, and would not let a tree be cut down.

We went home full of our discovery. What a place to spend the summer in — birds nesting all about you, and an atmosphere of peace and quietness that would rest the most wearied soul. It seemed a Garden of Eden. We afterwards learned that the woman had been *branded* by her husband — with a red-hot iron cattle brand — because she refused to keep his saddle in her parlor! The husband was a fine-looking man of more than ordinary intelligence, shrewdness, and cruelty. Years ago he was convicted as one of the ringleaders in the Mountain Meadow Massacre, and a bounty was offered for his head. Forced to flee from Utah, he sought refuge in northern Arizona, where, on the outskirts of the dreaded " Painted Desert " he built houses for two of his wives at distant points in a secluded cañon and lived in comparative comfort, beyond the reach of officers of the law. Last year in a quarrel over pasturage for his horses, he was killed by a Navajo Indian.

VIII.

THE BROWNIES.

There were two droll little boys constantly going back and forth through our yard, doing errands and " chores " for the lonely old grandmother across the street. Brownies, I dubbed them, from their quaint humorous air, and the thoughtful way in which they looked after the old grandmother.

One brownie had an upturned nose and incredulous black eyes; the other, sleek yellow hair and mild blue eyes. They both wore comical old men's black felt hats down over their noses, and manly suspenders girded over their tattered shirts.

After our first conversation they regarded me as a jocose person, and as they passed my chair, their staid gravity would suddenly give way and they would burst out laughing.

They were amusing mixtures of child and man. They worked as steadily as if they had seen threescore instead of scarce ten summers — these quaint little old men. They hoed their grandmother's garden, striking the ground with comical little manly strokes; they then used their hoe handles as wands to swing themselves over the ground.

They usually looked ashamed when surprised in any such childishness, but one day they quite forgot that they were men. The blue-eyed brownie had a toothache and his mother was away. He came to us with his swelled cheek bound by a red bandana under his old man's black hat, and his eyes puffed out by real child's tears.

His small brother followed him about in helpless distress, and stood by when the little sufferer applied a stinging lotion, asking with a child's awed sympathy, "Does it hurt much?"

In their distress the tiny old men even let me tell them stories. And when the pain was eased, one tired little workman brownie curled himself down on our steps, laid his head on his tattered sleeve, and was soon fast asleep — the poor little weary child, trying so hard to do the work of a man.

In the summer, the brownies became hay-makers, working more like farmers than ever. I hoped that they sometimes stole a game of hide-and-seek, and was relieved to find them running over to their grandmother's between loads, to shake some green apples from her trees.

IX.

GRANDMA.

The brownies' faithful care of the old grandmother, and the sight of the troop of little grandchildren carrying flowers to the old grandfather's grave, gave me a tender interest in the poor old lady, who, they said, was "grieving" so sorely in the little house behind the trees across the street.

The old people had been married "most sixty years," our school-teacher told me, "and they were never separated but two days in all that time — when grandpa went to see his son in Salt Lake."

Now the little grandmother was left alone. It was too late to uproot her, she could never be content even in her children's homes; so they went to take care of her in the old house. I was touched by the thoughtful tenderness with which they cherished her. Her daily cup of tea was carried over — " so mother won't have to build a fire at noon — it's so hot ; " at the baking an extra loaf was set to rise " so she won't have to bake ; " some one went to sit with her at her lonely meals, " she misses father so, to eat alone ; " and she was never left long by herself in the desolate house, " she grieves so, all the time."

When I went to see her, I found her in her little kitchen. There were two big rocking-chairs, one on either side the stove — one empty now. A pathetic old pipe still lay on the mantelpiece, an old hat and coat still hung against the wall; later, her children put them tenderly out of her sight. " I could n't bear them," the dear old soul said, tremulously.

" He was so kindly to me," she sobbed, when telling me of her desolation. " He was so kindly to me — always so kind. Since I was took with the lameness — two year this April — he always had my stockings warm for me in the morning —

always so kind. Oh! nobody knows, nobody knows *the miss of it!*" she cried out in her loneliness.

When less borne down by her grief she rambled on about their happy life together. All her memories of sixty years were bound up with the thought of "father." She told me that when the old man used to go out in the yard, the hens would all follow him, — seventy-five or more, — and the neighbors going by would stop at the fence and laugh.

Then her mind would wander back to the early days of their married life in England, and she would recall with tender pleasure how, "before I had any children, my husband would bring me young birds and lambs, for I always wanted something young — always must have something to love."

She told me how rich they might have been if her husband had gone to Australia to raise sheep — " he was always such a hand with sheep." But the Mormon missionary found them, and they came to America. " Not all the gold in California," the old lady said impressively, — "not all the gold in California would have taken us from our home, but we come for the gospel, and so were happy in doing right;" and her beautiful face bore out the testimony.

She had had a remarkably varied and interesting life, and I liked to get her to talk about it when I went to sit with her. At first she used to ask me to go into the front room where the "Book of Mormon" lay on the centre-table, and a bust of Brigham Young stood on the mantelpiece. But I preferred the spotless sunny kitchen, where I could draw up my big rocker opposite hers, and watch her dear old face as she talked.

Her smooth white hair fell in curls beside her cheeks under bunches of purple flowers that decorated her black English cap. After all her troubles not a line of her face bespoke impatience or complaint — the record was of a life of loving-kindness. What she said made little difference to me. When she ran on with the garrulousness of old age, it was enough simply to sit and look at her serene old face.

When telling about England, her old eyes lit up with memories of her girlhood; and she fell easily into the quaint English dialect when talking to her family, though with me she rarely used the old expressions.

She had lived in one of the watering places frequented by the royal family, and it had been a familiar sight of her childhood to see Queen Victoria, herself a child then, riding her donkey about the hills — "Oh, such a handsome donkey!"

When in her teens, she had been lady's maid for a child of the royal family. "Lady —— always dressed me in Swiss muslin. The footmen in livery waited on us, and we waited on the ladies," she told me with pride; exclaiming, " Oh, I tell them I've been with the highest and I've been with the lowest — with the royal family and in a tent on the plains."

Her stories of court life were like pictures from an old novel. One romance she liked to dwell on. A handsome headstrong boy of noble blood had fallen in love with a wealthy tradesman's daughter who was visiting the baths; and on the spot he swore he would marry no one else. Grandma evidently had a soft spot in her heart for the handsome boy who had confided his love affairs to her fifty years ago, and it was interesting to hear her talk about him and the "beautiful lady," and wonder why it should be a sorrow to his family to have him marry her; though she moralized that there was a difference between the real gentry and the rich trades-folk; you could tell by the way they treated their servants, the nobles were so simple and kind.

After she left court life and had married the tollgatherer, and her boy was a baby, the royal physician came to get her to nurse a "great heir." She recited with a touch of pride the interviews with the grand personages, telling how the "great physician" begged, and the "dowager" cajoled, and how she refused with spirit at first, only compromising at last on half her time, because, "I would n't starve my baby for nobody."

Her native independence, increased perhaps by her American life, made it possible for her to criticise hesitatingly the customs of the "gentry," whom she still held in reverence. She told with disapproval how the mother of "the great heir" came into the grand nursery merely to pass down orders about her child, never offering to take her little one in her own arms. "She was no mother," the dear old grandmother concluded, sadly.

With her next breath, however, she would tell me how she used to dress her little girls in their pretty pink and blue frocks, and when "the great ladies" would drive by, they would stop to admire the pretty children. She remembered with pleasure that Lady ——, whose maid she had been, once came to see her, and actually drove to the apothecary's herself for a lotion she found was needed.

She liked to tell me about the old English customs, the church fasts and feasts; the day when "the clubs walked," — a procession of some society that carried gilt-headed clubs and walked past the castle gates to the church; after the service joining in the games and merry-making

She said there was great strife among the carol singers to see who would get to the house first on Christmas morning, for the one who came first got the best present.

It was considered bad luck to have a girl come first, she said. After she came to Utah, two girls "came first," one year. "They did not mean any harm, but came on an errand; and though father went down cellar and cut them a rasher of bacon, he always said we had bad luck all that year — our girl died that year." "There may not be anything in it," the old lady acknowledged, "but I love to see a boy come first."

When I looked through the window at the new moon she shook her head with disapproval — it was bad luck to see it through glass. "Father used to laugh at me and tell me it was an old woman's notion, but he would call me outside to look at the moon."

In her old English home there had been

a tradition of a neighborhood giant who had "fallen in the moat and been drowned." "I could n't say as it was so," she confessed, but the dear old soul evidently had a relish for the tale.

She loved to talk about the "shady lanes" of England, and the "nightingale that used to sing in our yard. Father and I used to listen to it moonlight nights," she recalled tenderly; adding, "There is n't any here; you don't have them here. Father used often to say, 'Oh, there is no nightingale here.'" Again and again, she told me with a smile that when they left England, "on the 26th of March, the sweetbriar hedges were in bloom."

She liked to remember the voyage over. "I love the sea," she exclaimed, with a noble light in her eyes. "We had a terrible storm, but no Latter-Day Saint was ever lost at sea, which shows that we were guided and blest — does n't it?" she confused me by asking, in her sweet straightforward way.

It was like reading a page of history to

hear her tell about crossing the plains. At Iowa they left the railroad and took to emigrant wagons. Their company was a wealthy one of fifty teams, and they had a merry time in crossing the plains. Even after traveling all day they were not too tired to dance at night. "We had splendid singers in our band," grandma said with a smile of pleasure at the memory of those happy days. But it was not all brightness. They met with one of the tragedies so common in pioneer life — their oxen stampeded and killed a number of women and children. Grandma pressed her own children thankfully to her heart, and the mourners buried their dead on the lonely plain and went on their way.

Grandma came over with a rich "Independent Company," but one day while I was sitting with her, an old woman came in and told us her experiences with a "hand-cart company;" one of the poorer companies that walked and drew part of their baggage in hand carts instead of having it carried by ox teams.

As the woman was very lame — just out of a hospital — she did not draw a cart as the other women did, though she walked most of the way.

She had a thrilling story to tell, and we drew up our chairs to listen, grandma often breaking in with some sympathetic explanation or pertinent question suggested by her own experience.

The company made their first five hundred miles very comfortably, walking about fifteen miles a day. But then a herd of buffalo stampeded the oxen, and they were forced to put cows before the wagons, transferring part of the baggage to the already loaded hand carts.

At Laramie, where they had expected to find provisions, they found nothing but a few barrels of sea biscuit. The company had left Iowa too late. They reached the mountains to find them deep under winter snows, and they had to go on with insufficient clothing for the cold weather, and with systems enfeebled by low rations.

"At last we got so that we had only

fourteen ounces apiece, for a three days' allowance. Some of the people boiled raw hide and ate it."

"Yes, I know you did," grandma exclaimed sympathetically.

"How did it taste?" I asked.

"I ate it once, and I never wanted any more," she replied.

"We slept in the snow," she explained, and, when I exclaimed in horror, added ironically, "*Snow* is warm. You get up in the morning and there is a steam around you. The only way I kept from freezin' in the daytime was by taking the blankets I slept in and wrapping them around my shoulders. Eleven froze to death in one night." Seventy died in all. Those who survived became so hardened from suffering, they were hardly like human beings. "The sight of a dead dog would be more to me now than a dead man then," the poor woman told us. She said, "I saw a woman fall dead at table and her husband go on eating as if nothing had happened."

"Oh! you suffered shockin'," grandma cried with a sad shake of the head; mourning, "Such hardships as the Mormons have been through!" Brigham Young sent out a rescuing party as soon as he heard how late they started, but when it reached them, nearly a fifth of their company were already dead. The early emigrants found Utah very different from the country they had left. Grandma told me how they suffered. "It was a wilderness of sage-brush" then, she said, — "nothing but sage-brush!" But still she spoke no word of complaint. "It was all different from anything we'd been used to," she said patiently.

The house grandma came to from her spacious English home had but two rooms and was covered with a mud roof. "Father used to say it rained hardest after the rain was over," she said to an old neighbor, and he nodded his head emphatically, exclaiming, "That it did — that it did."

The mud dropped down on grandma's white counterpanes — she had never seen colored patchwork quilts till she came to America, she told me with pride; they seemed so "curious" when she first saw them.

Under the dripping mud roofs there was no place for the fine linen she had brought from England, and the settlers were in great need of clothing; so she consented to sell them some of hers. "The women told me they had never seen so many white blankets," she said with housewifely satisfaction, adding, "and you know they were no good to me then. The women gave me a great deal of gold for my clothes. There were no four-posted bedsteads here, so I took my fine white dimity curtains, and had them dyed to make dresses for my girls."

The "plague" of grasshoppers came soon after grandma came to Utah. The men went out in bands and made ditches, into which they drove the grasshoppers, making the young hop into open sacks. "If they lay their eggs with us, we've got to support them," grandma explained.

After the "plague" came the "famine," when the crops having been destroyed, the starving settlers had to go "down on the bottoms for roots," and up in the mountains for service berries and the bulbs of the sago lily. "They ate everything of the vegetation," grandma declared, — "everything."

Money could buy little in those days. "The first pound of sugar I bought," she said, raising her forefinger and shaking it emphatically, — "the first pound of sugar I bought I paid one dollar for; and I did n't think it was much of a pound, either." She paid the dollar willingly, however, for "father was sick and could n't eat, but said to me, 'I think I could eat a *cup of sop*,'" — an old country mixture of sugar and bread and milk.

The dear old lady's rambling talk threw strong side lights on the way in which she took up this new life, accepting uncomplainingly all that was strange and hard; bravely carrying the burdens of her whole family; and going out to minister to her neighbors whose sufferings were greater than her own.

Once a terrible snowstorm overwhelmed the village, and for two days she and her family had to stay in bed to keep from freezing. Even then her little children grew chilled in her arms. Her mother's heart was full of dread and anguish, but she kept up the courage of her husband, and quieted the little ones, hiding her tears from them. "I never let him see me cry," she said protectingly of father — "that would have distressed him." In the same way in going about among the sick of the village she would "never tell them how sick they looked, the way some folks do, but always tried to cheer them up."

Her loving heart was ready to respond to any appeal. At Christmas time in the year of the "plague," she found a poor sick neighbor grieving because she had nothing for her children for Christmas. "I could n't have it that those children should n't have anything in their stockings," she said; so she came home, baked some little

English cakes at night, and filled their stockings with cakes and apples. "I think one of the girls was hearkening, but the rest did n't know," — smiling at the memory, — "and the mother never forgot it."

"Everybody in the village loved grandpa and grandma," our school-teacher told us. And I could see the respect that must have been mingled with that love. The old lady spoke with kindly sympathy to the old serving-woman to whom she sold her eggs, but the woman asked their price with timid deference. Even now there was a touch of authority and a strain of simple dignity in her bearing. When her little grandsons, the brownies, came into her kitchen, they stood behind the stove with their hats in their hands, abashed before the little white-haired grandmother. She held a position of dignity in the neighborhood. She was the mother of a respected race — thirty great-grandchildren blessed her memory. She had lands and cattle, and kept her private accounts, holding in mind the business of "the estate."

But mixed with her sound common sense and ability were the sterling virtues of a noble old English woman, while her whole nature was beautified by the deeply religious spirit that enabled her to idealize the gospel of Mormonism.

Her homely piety was touching in its simplicity. One day, when the family had left her in our care, I went over to sit with her at her lonely meal. The scene reminded me of a picture by one of the old Dutch painters. She drew her rocking-chair to the table, in her little kitchen, and spreading her loaf, bowed her dear white head and prayed, not a meaningless grace, but a fervent prayer for pardon for " sins thy pure eyes see." Afterwards, without a word, she raised her head and quietly began her meal.

She had been brought up in the Church of England, and in talking with her you might have thought her merely a devout believer in the Christian doctrines. The Book of Mormon and the words of Joseph Smith and Brigham Young had been merely added to the faith of her childhood.

In telling me of her happy life with father, she said: "At eight o'clock we would have prayers, and then he would take his light and go to bed, and at nine I would shut up the stove and follow. My husband used to talk about the judgment day, when we'd be sitting here at night alone in the dark. He'd say it would be a wonderful time of great joy and great sorrowing, when we come up to be judged for the deeds done in the body, good or evil. He used to talk beautiful about it," the dear old wife said reverently.

Then she wandered on, as we sat in the twilight, talking about life and death and her faith. "It is such a short time here," she said; "life is so short — seems as though but a breath — and then there is all eternity. I never could have borne what I have — lost my children — my Alice," — her voice always grew tremulous when she spoke of this daughter; "and now the great trial — separated from my beloved husband," her voice breaking, "I never could have borne it all if it had not been for my hope, my *great* hope."

X.

DOCTRINES OF THE LATTER-DAY SAINTS.

No one familiar with the origin and development of the religious systems of the world marvels at the phenomenon of Mormonism, even existing as it does in the heart of a Gentile country — a drop of sluggish mediæval blood in the heart of the United States.

Although this old world sect exists in the midst of modern civilization, it is surrounded by a Chinese wall of ignorance, church organization, and priestly control. As it is besieged by modern thought, and its guards are weakened by apostasy, its forces are recruited from the old world, from a class saturated with middle age traditions and superstitions. But already the siege is pressing hard, and silent squads are evacuating in the night, to take refuge in the more congenial civilizations of Canada and Mexico. The past cannot withstand the future.

The Mormon leaders made the mistake of founding the sect in a new progressive country. Utah was a wilderness of sagebrush then, but it is between Denver and San Francisco now, and the leaders can no longer control their environment. An early Mormon geography taught that all outside of Utah was desert and wilderness, where Indians and wild beasts roamed, and no Mormon child must ever venture. Now the public schools are teaching different lessons. Gentiles are settling among the Saints, whose sons and daughters are even venturing to marry outside the church. Under such conditions the whole Mormon system will have to be reorganized.

It was built up to appeal to the emigrant class, not to the intelligent American citizen. For its purpose, it was most cleverly adapted. Its founders, men of acute intelligence, used the peasant class as plastic material to further their own designs. To the emigrants, miracle and marvel were commonplace fact, submission to authority was a natural part of life. Unquestioning faith in the miraculous life of Joseph Smith, the Prophet, came readily from them, and, as readily, unquestioning submission to the authority of the church.

In formulating the doctrines of the church, the greatest emphasis was thrown upon the two points that would most effectually bring the mass of the people under the control of the leaders, — the Old Testament system of religious organization, and the divine relationships of the heads of the Mormon church. Many remarkable stories are told of the use to which Brigham Young put his celestial connection. At one time, it is said, he received, by mistake, an enormous consignment of green paint; and immediately proceeded to have a revelation that the faithful should mark their abodes — as the Israelites of old — by painting their gates green; charitably consenting to sell them the paint, and flattering them by their close relation to heaven.

This system of direct revelation was given plausibility by referring it back to the Old Testament prophets. Indeed, great cleverness was shown in elaborating the Mormon doctrines. There was little to startle or antagonize. The Bible was still the foundation of the creed. The words used were those the people had reverenced from childhood up. To those who had never had any vivid sectarian faith, it came as a revival of their vague Christianity. The Prophet Joseph had come to arouse them. The Old Testament prophets had been true prophets; Christ had been the Son of God; but his followers had been men. They had misread his words, they had founded false church systems. Grieved at this, God had at last sent the Prophet Joseph to build a true church; restoring with him the lines of the priesthoods of Aaron and Melchizedek, that the new church might be kept from the errors of the old by direct communication of its priests with heaven; and so the earth be prepared for his second coming.

Sympathy and reverence for Joseph Smith were aroused by the parallels drawn at all points between his life and that of Christ; from the miracles that were part of his daily life, through his "persecution" and final "martyrdom."

The Mormon creed contains much that is found in all Christian articles of faith, together with an unfamiliar emphasis of church organization and the authorization of revelations. The familiar parts of the creed cover belief in the Trinity, faith in Christ, a literal resurrection, repentance, belief in works and faith, and in the Bible as the word of God "as far as correctly translated." Less familiar is the belief in the Book of Mormon as the word of God, side by side with the Bible; in salvation through baptism, by immersion; belief in the organization of the primitive church, — in apostles, prophets, pastors, teachers, evangels; and in the gift of tongues, healing, prophecy, and revelation. The creed not only registers a belief in all that has been and is revealed, but announces that still more will be revealed about the kingdom of God; that there will be a literal gathering of Israel and a restoration of the ten tribes; that Zion will be built upon this continent; that Christ will reign personally upon the earth, which will be renewed and receive its paradisaic glory.

The church organization is based upon that of the apostles and prophets. A President, who is " a seer, revelator, translator, and prophet," presides over the whole church. Then come the two orders of Priesthood: The Melchizedek priests, who receive revelations and enjoy spiritual blessings, are divided into Apostles, Seventies, Patriarchs or Evangelists, and Elders. The Aaronic priests, who "hold the keys of administering angels, and administer the outward ordinances of the church," are divided into Bishops, Priests, Teachers, and Deacons. Besides these, there are the Quorum of the First Presidency, the Twelve Apostles, the High Council, the Seventies, the High Priests, the Elders, and the Quorum of the Lesser Priesthood.

By means of this elaborate system, the heads of the church have complete control of the mass of the people. Nothing happens without their knowledge, and it is said that an order transmitted from the President will reach every Mormon in Utah within a week; and that, without an outsider's being aware of any movement.

XI.

THE PRACTICE OF THE DOCTRINES.

Upon the matter of church organization and the inner workings of the system, a casual visitor in Utah, like myself, gets little light; but by talking with the people, I got an idea of the way in which many of the Mormon doctrines are put in practice.

To an outsider, one of the most appalling features of Mormonism is the rooted opposition of the people to medical science, their distrust of the skilled physician, and their faith in the Biblical ceremonials of anointing and laying on of hands. In the younger generation both the prejudice and the faith are being modified, even Brigham Young having taught that the church ceremonials should be supplemented by medicine; but in talking with grandma I found the old faith unshaken. She told me with reverent memories of the help she had received. At one time when she had been ill so long that she had lost all courage and hope, the Mormon sisters had her brought into Salt Lake. As she was too sick to go through the Temple to be healed, they said that they would "administer" to her; and taking sacred oil they bathed and anointed her, praying over her during the ceremony. "Oh, the words was beautiful," she exclaimed, with an exalted look in her dear old eyes.

When the administration was concluded they said to her impressively, "Sister, your mission is not ended yet. If this does not make you well, something will come to you that will help you." And the dear soul, full of unquestioning faith told me how she went home and soon after found a patent medicine circular on the floor, — no one ever knew where it came from, and she believed it was "sent." So father went down street and got a bottle for her, and that was the first thing that helped her.

At another time she had been too ill to go to the conference held in the village, so the holy elders of the church came up and blessed her, administering the "laying on of hands;" and she "began to get well from that day."

When a christening occurred in the village, grandma explained to me the rites of baptism. She said, "We don't call it christening, we call it blessing the babies." It seems that, according to the Mormon customs, when the child is eight days old its father ought to bless and name it. Then on a fast day,—they come on the first Thursday of every month,—the baby is blessed and named by the Elders, with laying on of hands. At eight years old, the child is baptized and confirmed.

Baptism with the Mormons means immersion, and grandma told me that young girls were often baptized in the village pond when the ice had to be broken for them; and that afterwards they had to drive two or three miles in their wet clothing. When I exclaimed in horror, she explained that they were " wrapped in shawls and quilts " and the men " drove as fast as they could ; " and she assured me that " none of them ever catches a bit of cold." I thought sadly of the number of young girls who have died from consumption as the direct result of such criminal disregard of the laws of health ; but I held my peace.

Baptism and the ceremonies of the church, such as confirmation and marriage, are often held in the Temple now. Grandma's face lit up with a holy light when she spoke of the sacred edifice. When I asked her what it was like, she said, "I can't *describe* it, but it is the *beautifullest* place — white — with correspondences — so beautiful ! "

From a Mormon who was half "apostate," I heard more of the Temple. She said she was " no traitor," but she could give me a hint of the meaning and magnificence of the wonderful building, as it had impressed her. It is modeled on Solomon's Temple, and fitted up inside with the utmost splendor; ebony, marble, and alabaster being seen on every hand; while the doors are studded with precious stones sent by the faithful, from the mines of South America, Africa, and all parts of the earth where the Mormon converts have wandered.

There is one main court, like a church, at the upper end of which stand twelve life-size gilded oxen, upholding the great baptismal font. Then there are large assembly chambers for the Bishops and Seventies, for the heads of the church: "rooms where they can meet in troublous times to consult as to the wisest ways to induce a right spirit among the people."

The symbolism of the Temple — what grandma probably meant by "correspondences" — is developed in a series of connecting rooms. First comes one representing the Garden of Eden — the four walls are painted in each room like a cyclorama. Here, all is peace and happiness, "the lion and the lamb lying down together" in the green beautiful garden; and the other animals feeding harmoniously together. In the room leading out of this, everything is changed. Sin has been introduced by Adam's fall. Conflict and horror rage; the lion tears the lamb in pieces, the beasts fall on each other in fury. It is a vivid picture of the "struggle for existence," I was surprised to hear the Mormon woman say. The sky is lurid with tempest, but in one corner of the room the clouds are lightened, the sky is softened — here a door leads into the room symbolizing the "first glory." What these glories are, my friend could not tell me, but I imagined from what she said that they were stages in the development of the world, through Mormonism, from the unregenerate days of the struggle for life before Joseph Smith, to the attainment of the highest Mormon heaven — the "celestial glory" — open only to faithful followers of the Prophet.

Altogether the Temple must be a wonderfully impressive building, for this apostate, whose mind was torn between Mormonism and Theosophy, who said she did not know one day what she would believe the next, — even she told me with awed voice that it was wonderful, that one must be better for merely passing through it.

None but the faithful are now admitted to the temple, and they only when they bring certificates of good character from their bishops; and when they have "work to do." This "work" grandma explained to me very vividly. The theory seems to be that each Mormon family should try to give its ancestors the opportunity to embrace Mormonism. "There is no compulsion," grandma said in her sweet way, unwilling to obtrude her faith; but as she talked, she drew her chair closer to mine in her earnestness, hoping, the dear old soul, that her words might perhaps open to me the joys of the "celestial glory." Each family wishes to complete its line from Adam down, to bring all of its race within the church, so that finally, when the Mormons are gathered together in the "celestial glory," none of their ancestors shall be among the unregenerate to be destroyed from off the earth. "As there is no repentance in the grave, the work must be done on this earth." For the Saints give their ancestors the opportunity to become Mormons by proxy baptisms and confirmations — by "working for the dead." They get the names of their ancestors from the old gravestones in the churchyards of Europe. Grandma said that she had known people to work for seventy of their ancestors in a day — a profitable enthusiasm for the church, each baptism costing two dollars.

I asked grandma if people were baptized for the children, and she said that those under eight had no sins, that "Christ died for them," — a singular modification of the Christian doctrine.

When talking of the "work," grandma said earnestly, "It is the most beautifullest work that was ever done on earth — since Christ was here — of course the same thing was done then. It can never all be done in this world till the millennium, the thousand years when Christ will be on the earth; but there won't be any other work to do then but that in the temples," she concluded meditatively.

In describing the work to me, her face took on its most beautiful expression. She said the workers all wear Temple robes of white — men and women all are robed in white as they form in procession, walking two by two, up to the great baptismal font, that is upheld by the golden oxen. Sometimes hundreds of white-robed workers will be standing around the font waiting to be baptized. She said devoutly, "It makes me think of the Judgment Day."

"Father and I have done all we could," she said reflectively, "but my children will have a great deal of work to do — there will be a great deal of work for them to do, for I cannot do it now — my strength is not great enough now. And they will do it," she added confidently, "they will be happy in doing it."

XII.

POLYGAMY.

The Mormons are now passing through a transition stage in the practice of polygamy. Theoretically, the practice has been abolished; but while it is reasonable to imagine that the law has reduced the number of annual polygamous marriages, the law requiring old polygamists to give up all but their first wives is openly disregarded. It would be strange indeed if such a law were obeyed; for it is manifestly one of the cases where retrogressive legislation is unjust. It is true that the government built a home for the wives who were to be abandoned, but that hardly affects the question. It seems rather a refinement of cruelty to make amends for breaking up a woman's home, by sending her to the almshouse. What the law has done is this: it has put a premium on bribery, hypocrisy, and deceit. At one time the administration became so rotten that when the marshal died, one of our village polygamists openly boasted that he no longer had to pay tithes to him.

As there were about thirty polygamists in our village, the different effects of the law were well illustrated. One woman of strong character was supporting herself, against the wishes of her husband, because she was a second wife and would not break the law by living with him; on the other hand, one of the Mormon elders had obeyed the law by going to Canada with his young second wife, leaving the old mother of his children behind, — these being different forms of conscientiousness.

Another prominent member of the Church of the Saints, who had six living wives, came under government notice and had to fly to the mountains, where he was hunted by the officers for two years. When he was found, however, a number of wealthy Gentile business connections petitioned for his pardon, stipulating that he should take his oath to abide by the law. Whereupon being duly sworn, he returned to his six wives, no further questions being asked. One of the village government officials had two wives, but although the Salt Lake Tribune reported the case, nothing was done about it.

Indeed, disregard of the law was a matter of such common knowledge that when the present marshal was installed, a bishop went to ask him if he meant to enforce the law; and when told that he did, remarked quietly that it would be pretty hard on his people, but he would let them know.

In talking with the villagers we were much interested in their arguments for polygamy. Like most of the doctrines of the Latter-Day Saints, it was shown to be merely a natural and righteous return to the customs sanctioned by the Old Testament. Moreover, they urged that it was advocated by the New Testament, some even going so far as to state that Christ himself was a polygamist, Mary and Martha being his wives! Some of the women seem to have accepted it merely on these grounds.

One of those I talked with, however, had never thought the matter out, but she was a monogamist. When I asked her the theory of polygamy, she said, —

"It will give greater glory."

"Why?" I urged. "What is the idea of the church?"

"I don't know, I have never read up on that; but it is a doctrine of the church, *the main doctrine of the church*," pushed, perhaps, by my insistence to an acknowledgment of what many deny.

"Then you believe in it because it is a doctrine of the church, not from any idea of your own about it?"

"Yes, it is a doctrine of the church. That is to say," she added, as if realizing that she had committed herself by acknowledging it to be the *chief* doctrine of the Mormons, — "that is, it says in the Book of — the revelation of Joseph Smith, that *polygamy is right as long as it is not against the law of the land.* I have read that in the Book of — myself;" and she completed her withdrawal by saying conclusively, "Of course, now that it is against the law of the land, they don't do it!"

One old woman, better acquainted with the theories of the Mormon leaders, practically acknowledged that polygamy was instituted for the more rapid increase of the sect.

Some of the better class of women tried to bring its warrant from abstract ethical principles. They held that it was not only sanctioned by nature, but made society purer, and was right "as a means of grace," because it developed the Christian character. One of the most intelligent and cultured Salt Lake Mormon women told an acquaintance of mine that as love developed with married life, it expanded the nature so that the husband could love more than one wife, and the wife could love the other wives and their children in a truly Christian way; and that a polygamous family developed the characters of all, as a large family of children develop more unselfishly than an only child. She said to my friend, "On that spot where your chair is, my husband has stood to take four wives!" And she insisted earnestly that it had been at her desire.

When discussing polygamy with grandma, she said, "When it is done right, it is a beautiful thing, and them that have done it right shall have great glory." Her daughter, who was in the room at the time, exclaimed fervidly, —

"Yes, I have seen some families in which it was just beautiful. The wives lived like sisters, and the children just the same. It was 'Auntie this,' and 'Auntie that;' and if any of the children was sick — oh, it was just beautiful."

"Do you think the majority of the men take their wives from a sense of duty?" I asked innocently.

"Yes, it is often very hard for them — they hate to do it."

"They do it for righteousness' sake,"

dear old grandma broke in, with her usual idealizing spirit.

"Then you think a man had just as soon marry an ugly old woman as a pretty young girl," I said, pressing the matter.

"Yes, as long as a woman is good and respectable, that is all," the daughter declared; adding warmly, as if to prove to her own conscience the statement the heat of the discussion had forced from her,—

"I knew a man in ——, as pretty a man as I ever see, married the ugliest old women! Yes, I know it is so." I thought of the men who go to Canada with their favorite young wives, leaving the old ones in Utah; but I went on calmly.

"How should you like to see your husband make love to another woman?"

"Oh, but they don't," she declared. "They love the first wife dearly. They can't love two women alike. They marry for religion."

"Then they love only one wife?" I demanded. "Isn't that pretty hard on the others? How terrible it would be to marry a man who did not love you!"

"Oh, they bear it for the sake of religion!" she concluded, quite borne to the wall by the argument.

"Then you think polygamy makes suffering," I pursued relentlessly. "It isn't done without suffering?"

"Oh, no," she conceded, "but they will have great glory."

Grandma, at another time, made the same acknowledgment. Indeed, I did not talk with any one who denied that it caused suffering. Grandma said, "It is a great trial for the women," but added with a touch of her droll humor, "And for the men too." I thought of the polygamist whose domestic tragedies I had stumbled on in looking for a saddle, and smiled intelligently.

One old white-haired woman told a pathetic story. She began by saying that when she was married, she did not know anything about polygamy. Then, correcting herself, she asked, "What did I say that for? Of course I knew about it, but," pathetically, "I didn't suppose it would ever have to come to *me*." Then she went on to tell how her husband took two other wives " and brought them home to me. He took them in the right spirit," she declared loyally, — the church often ordered men to take more wives when they would not do it voluntarily, — but afterwards one of them, with whom he was now living in Canada, had alienated his affections from her, and when the old wife's children were dying — she lost seven of her ten — he was acting the part of lover to this young wife. " I felt it so hard when I was losing my children," the poor old woman cried.

Nevertheless, she said she knew the ordinance was right, and so had tried to put the bitter thoughts out of her heart. When asked why it was right she said, " Because Joseph Smith had a revelation that it was." " You don't believe that Joseph Smith was a Prophet," she said, " but I *know* he was." Then she went on, saying that " when they did it in the right spirit and the right way, it was right ;

but it was because they did n't, that it became almost a curse to us, and so a law was made against it."

Another woman made the same acknowledgment. She said, referring it back in true Mormon fashion, "The Prophets overdone it as we have." But when I asked her if she meant that they took too many wives, she was startled at her own admission. She conceded, however, that when a man can support only one wife and takes more, it is bad. As a matter of fact, I was told that the additional wives usually supported themselves, enabling their husband to take his ease on the street corners.

Whatever may have been the results to character "when it was done right," the obvious ordinary results were very far from being a "means of grace." The saintly instincts of some women were doubtless developed by it; but in the average undisciplined woman, it could arouse only "hatred, malice, and all uncharitableness." In the vaunted case of the two wives who dressed alike, and were said to be "like sisters," I was told that "one had the look of a broken heart," and the other "had spells of being possessed by the evil spirit."

Another woman, a Mormon who had lived among the Mormons for years, but who no longer believed "the married part" of the religion, told me of a number of cases where Christian graces were not developed by polygamy. She had known one old woman who became so much attached to a young girl she thought she would like to have her husband marry her, and he did so. When the two came back from their wedding, my informant told me in her graphic way, the old wife had the table set for their supper, but when she met them at the door, she turned white, and cried out, "You go, I can never see you again," and talked as if going wild; and many of them do "go wild," poor heart-broken creatures that they are.

The Mormon told me of one case where the first wife's bitterness reached such a point that she declared she would make her husband take a third wife, that the second one might suffer what she had.

My friend knew what it meant herself. In the old country, she told me, the missionary said very little about polygamy. But when he heard them discussing it among themselves, he explained to them that "things were so different in America that when they got there the spirit of the Lord would come between them and their husbands and they would feel all right about it." He said to my friend, "The trouble with you is that you have a pretty man and are a little jealous." And the good woman went on to say that when she got to Utah "there was a woman who thought a great deal of my husband for a good while; but I may say," she concluded fervidly, "that the spirit of the Lord never came to our house."

At another time, in her dramatic foreign way, she told me the details of the story. She said the woman "made up" to her husband till he really thought of taking her for a second wife. "I asked him how he'd like me to take the children and leave him, and he said he'd sooner die than that; and I said I would if he did n't quit, — and he quit. I put it to him, how would he like to have a young pretty man come in and sit down by the lamp, and me talk nice to him and be in love with him; and he sit and listen. He said that if it was the way for women to have more husbands, he supposed the men would have to stand it; but I told him if the *women* could n't bear it now, the *men* could n't — and he see how it was. He believed in it for a great many years, but he does n't now."

I told my friend that it was said the women liked polygamy. "You talk to them and you think they believe it," she acknowledged, "but I am *sure* they don't feel that way; and she told me of more cases that had come under her own knowledge showing the tragedies of polygamy. A young girl from the old country went to work for a rich Mormon lady in Salt Lake. The young girl sang at her work, but the lady was sad.

At last the little maid asked her mistress why she was sad, when she lived in a beautiful house and had all that money can buy.

"I have a broken heart," the lady answered.

"But you have a husband," the little maid said.

"You may say I *have* had one," the woman cried in anguish.

The other case was a girl of twenty who formed a "celestial marriage" with a man over seventy. "She did not know what love was, but thought it would give her heaven; she heard so much about it in preaching."

In this way polygamy has developed all the evil in the natures of the weak Mormon women, while it has made the best women do outrage to the most sacred instincts of womanhood, and accept the agony of martyrs in the blasphemous name of religion.

Originally, the Mormons established polygamy by a subtle appeal to what is worst in man and best in woman; and as long as the women believe that it is right, the laws can never crush it out. The spirit that is finest and best in woman — her power of self-sacrifice before abstract right — has been used as a tool of torture, and it will be used successfully until education teaches her that there is a higher light for her to follow.

We have not done our duty when we have passed a law forbidding her to do what she believes to be right; we will not have done our duty until we give her the education that will prove to her that our law forbids her to do wrong. And what will that education be? Surely not that which will enable her to still ignore the law of cause and effect, that will leave her with the faith that her diseases will be healed by the "laying on of hands;" that life is to be purified by any system that brutalizes men, destroys the sacredness of home, and crushes woman's noblest life with sacrilegious hands. No, the education that we owe to her is the highest and broadest that we have attained. It must develop her reasoning powers by the most careful scientific training, teaching her that the universe is governed by immutable laws, not set aside by revelations about green paint; enabling her to read the lessons of the historical development of the religious systems of the world with calm unprejudiced mind; and to recognize the futility of modeling the civilization of the future upon the outgrown institutions of the past; the danger of turning to the past for the ethical ideals of the future. For above all, it must teach her that the hope of the world lies in the evolution of moral and spiritual life.

XIII.

THE GREAT SALT LAKE.

When I stopped at Jumbo's home in the meadows, it was usually on my way to the "salt works" on the lake. With the first whiff of strong salt air, he and I were both ready for a gallop; and we loped merrily down to the lake.

Little was going on there. When the "Mollie Gibson" mine shut down in Colorado, the "salt works" were closed in Utah; for the salt was shipped to the mine, to be used in separating the ore. The "works" consisted of a small boiler house on the lake, whose engine pumped the lake water into ditches leading to excavated quadrangular ponds in which the water evaporated leaving the salt. When the salt formed three or four inches thick it was scraped up with shovels, packed into bags, and loaded into freight cars.

Jumbo and I used to climb the embankments of the ponds to march back and forth inhaling the invigorating salt air — so strong it made me lightheaded to breathe it rapidly — overlooking the beautiful snow-white ponds set against the exquisite blue of the lake.

On the shore near the salt works was a deserted bathing resort. Since it was built, the lake had receded, leaving it stranded high and dry, with a wide stretch of black mud between it and the lake. By going out a short distance, however, the bathing was comparatively clear, and as a German family were in charge of the resort, my friend and I used often to ride down on horseback.

We had always heard of the bathing in Salt Lake, but found it more peculiar than we had imagined. The bath-houses prepared us for some of the surprises awaiting us. Each room had its stationary bowl and faucet of fresh water, besides a fresh water shower bath; the necessity for which we understood after coming out of the lake with faces and hair frosted with salt, and after learning that our suits would be speedily rotted if we left any salt in them.

Each bathroom had a large printed notice warning bathers to beware of getting the lake water in " eyes, nose, or mouth," on account of its large percentage of salt, — a warning we soon appreciated. For it is dangerous to be sportive in this water. People are said to strangle from swallowing it, and we could readily believe it, so intense was the inflammation set up by a few tastes of it. We could easily understand the tonic effect we experienced from the baths.

The buoyant quality of the water is most astonishing. As you wade out in the shallows, at each step your feet are lifted for you. You can float in a little over a foot of water. Reclining on the lake bottom, you can keep your feet down only by a strong effort; while with your feet once off the bottom your body is gently buoyed up, and, behold, you are floating out to sea! I had never succeeded in swimming before, but found it an easy matter in that heavy water.

One day when we rode down to the lake, long rows of gulls were sitting on the beach; and when we went in bathing, we found a horde of snowy white spectators assembled on the shore. When we swam in shore towards them they did not pay much attention to us. But at last two of them rose, and flying over us turned and looked down at us from all sides like inspecting sentinels. Then, as I kept on toward the flock, suddenly, as if in response to a signal, the whole band rose and flew silently out over the lake.

Another day, when there was a haze in the air and the lake was like a mirror, I found a flock of gulls scattered over its smooth surface, sitting motionless as ducks. Swimming slowly and silently through the quiet water, I came so close I might have been numbered with them — another speck on the face of the lake. As I rested lightly on the buoyant water, breathing the warm dreamy air, my eyes on the level of the smooth lake, over whose surface midsummer insects were idly playing, my only companions the white birds around me, a sudden fancy came over me, and I gave myself up to its airy suggestions. I was one of their band, and could live with them on the still white lake. My world was a world of pearly water. Beyond my white sisters, over the face of the gray mirror, soft clouds were idly trailing. On my farthest horizon, hazy mountains rose dimly over my dreamland. Surely these were my sisters — they had let me join their snowy company. Sitting close around me, pluming their feathers or drowsing in the sun, they had taken me for one of their band. The fancy grew and possessed me till at last, when the white birds rose and flew away, I felt as if I should spread my wings and fly away after them — as if they had been cruel to leave me behind.

Our early morning rides to the lake, and our swim in the refreshing water, prepared us for the full enjoyment of the sunbaths we took before remounting our horses. On the white salt beach, with the blue water at my feet, I rested in the warm sun under the sky, rejoicing when a round white cloud came sailing in through the blue close above me. Twittering swallows circled low over me, dragon flies came to inspect me, snowy gulls crossed my blue screen — the world with its sin and sorrow was behind me — I rested in the stillness and peace of the beautiful lake.

Sometimes we rode down for our baths in the late afternoon, my friend carrying our supper in her botany can. Then we unsaddled our horses, and the good German took down a length of fence to let them graze in the inclosure surrounding the band stand; while we spread our meal in a vine-covered summer-house, picked green leaves for a mat for the red apples on our round table, and feasted merrily, drinking warm milk fresh from the milking. Then we remounted our horses, and leaving the crescent bay rimmed with gold, were ready for our cool ride home in the sunset.

One evening as we were watching the sunset from the pier, before turning homeward, the little German children came out for a romp in the lake. They took boards for rafts, and while the boys played near shore, their little sister drifted out on her boat. As the mountains were melting into a rich purple haze, the sun, sinking behind the lake, sent its slanting golden rays across the dark water, lighting up the little fair-haired maiden till she floated on a raft of gold.

While we watched the insects moving to and fro above the pier, the great golden harvest moon rose over the Wasatch. Opposite, across the lake, the afterglow was bright in the sky, and the rigging of an anchored boat stood out dark against the band of ruddy orange light. On another boat a sail was raised and rode slowly out across the lake. In the cool evening air, the calm beauty of the night touched our hearts. The great golden moon that had just risen over us had long been shining on our far away Eastern homes, and all through the still night it would shine over us and over them — over our living and over the graves of our dead.

XIV.

CLIMBING THE WASATCH WITH A PROFESSOR.

As our village was really in the desert belt of Utah, when the spring flowers were gone, my botanical friend found her material disappointing; and so, when the pioneer botanist of Utah invited us to join him on a collecting trip in the Wasatch, we hailed the opportunity with enthusiasm.

Although no botanist, I was eager for the trip. I had not lived under the shadow of the Wasatch all summer without longing to get back into the mountains; and it would have been a sore disappointment to have left the Territory with only a picture of their face. As we had just read Agassiz's Life, full of his glacial work, our enthusiasm ran high when we found that we were going among glacier-worn cañons.

The trip had a delightful mountain flavor from the outset — we were to meet the Professor in the Rio Grande Western station with tickets to Wasatch. We went to Salt Lake a day beforehand in order to catch the early morning train, and had been waiting impatiently at the station for some time when the preoccupied Professor came hurrying in, looking for us through his spectacles. He was hung with field glass, barometer, botany can and press, and after a few abstracted remarks to us, went out to watch over his dryers — a stack of brown pads that, to my astonished eyes, suggested a Saratoga trunk. With logic characteristic of a naturalist, he had considered his coat too bulky to carry — though we were bound for the snowy mountain tops. After a personal interview with the baggage man, the Professor concluded to let him take charge of the precious dryers — the baggage being merely partitioned off from the passenger end of our car.

The plan of our trip was to enter the Wasatch a few miles southeast of Salt

Lake City; climb the cañon — Little Cottonwood — on a tram; cross the divide separating it from Big Cottonwood, on horseback, coming down through Big Cottonwood cañon by stage to Salt Lake.

As I was more interested in geology than botany, in the short intervals between the discovery and discussion of flowers along the way, I tried to extract information about the geology of the mountains. Just before we entered the cañon, the Professor pointed out the famous earthquake fault, there a drop of sixty feet, which extended two hundred miles along the base of the range, and which, a geologist had hinted, was only a prophesy of an earthquake that should swallow up Salt Lake City itself.

On reaching Wasatch — the mountain village where the granite was quarried for the Temple — we saw perched on a terrace above us a most remarkable-looking conveyance. It proved to be our tram car — a hand car furnished with three wagon seats, each protected by a parasol-like blue and white striped awning. It was drawn up the cañon by two horses, tandem. It came down by gravity — and a brake. "Ben," the rear horse, put down his head and strained steadily, but the leader's tugs were often slack, and our driver's exhortations and admonitions were our accompaniment along the way. "Walk up, Dick!" "Get out of this, Dick!" he shouted with increasing emphasis; snapping his long clothesline-like whip at the leader with a louder and sharper snap as practice gave dexterity, his face growing tenser with exasperation.

The awnings protected us so effectually that we saw little along the way, except when we craned our necks to look at a suddenly opening view of the grand walls of the cañon. Fortunately for our serenity there was usually little to see, the tram car brushing through the green undergrowth of maple, elder, and cottonwood most of the way. Occasionally, in an interval between pointing out a rare plant or a glacial moraine, the Professor caught a bunch of choke-cherries as we passed.

The tram had been built to bring down ore from the Alta mines to the railroad at Wasatch. We reached Alta in time for dinner. It was an interesting type of a deserted mining camp. Opened in 1864, it was one of the oldest and richest silver mines in the Territory. When it had boasted three thousand inhabitants it was suddenly swept by fire; and now held but nine families, having, during the "silver trouble," but one open mine.

The superintendent of "the grizzly" and his assayer, who received us with great courtesy, were the only educated men in the place; and in winter, the superintendent went down to his family, leaving the young assayer cut off from the world.

"What do you do?" we asked.

"Oh, I've plenty of books," he answered quietly; but when pressed acknowledged that it was lonely. He brought out a pair of Norwegian snow-shoes — skees — fourteen feet long and six inches wide — his winter walking boots — his only means of going abroad. Pointing to the precipitous mountain wall opposite, he astonished us by saying that he had ridden down it on his skees. He could not fasten the snow-shoes to his feet, it would not be safe. It was dangerous, but exciting work, he said simply. He had been up and down most of the mountains around Alta.

The people had cut the trees from the steep sides of the cañon to use in the mines, leaving the town without protection, and a hundred men had been killed by snow slides. Six had been killed in the cellar of the assayer's house, he informed us calmly.

We spent the afternoon collecting flowers — that is, the Professor and my friend collected, and I — went along.

In the evening we visited the post office — a small compartment in a far corner of the camp store. The store having been stocked in the days of Alta's prosperity, its goods were now wearing out on the shelves. In more ways than one, the store echoed the former glories of the mining camp. In following the postmaster to his office, from the group of old drunken miners sitting telling yarns in the front part of the shop, we passed into the silent dimly lighted interior. In the back of the room was a bar filled with old black bottles under a sign of "Positively no Credit." From the bar we followed through a dark closet-like room with a large table, laid, presumably, with gambling counters. This opened into the post office, where the postmaster showed us with pride the hole where powder had been put to blow up his safe.

We did not find it difficult to believe that "Alta had been a hard place;" and we drew our own conclusions when we found a big revolver casually lying out on the table of the English family — to the care of whose good women my friend and I had been consigned. The next day, as we rode on up the trail, we looked back on the desolate town, moralizing sadly on the place the mining camp holds in our present civilization.

As we climbed toward the divide, our

trail often looked like a brown thread winding over the face of the mountain.

All the morning we rode through a veritable garden of flowers. They were astonishing, although the season had turned, and the Professor had nightmares lest those he was in search of had already been touched by the frost. To my unbotanical eye, the ride was a feast of color. There were exquisite clusters of blue flax, tall groups of white columbines of surpassing purity and beauty, rich purple monkshoods, luxuriant clumps of mertensias, of such delicate Frenchy pink and blue shading that my friend dreamed of them after she got home; besides the glowing " painted cups," and great stretches of yellow flowers, like patches of sunshine on the mountain sides. The Professor told us which flowers marked off the ascending life zones — for we found even Alpine plants, we went so high. But in my ignorance, I had soon forgotten the names; though I shall long remember a bowlder with a line of blue flowers blossoming out of a crack along its face.

As we stood on the divide, where the Professor's barometer registered an altitude of 10,250 feet and patches of snow were unmelted in August, we were silenced by the wonderful pictures in both directions below us. The grandest view was behind us. We looked back upon the bold peaked V walls of Little Cottonwood Cañon, and through the blue notch where Salt Lake valley lay in the distance. Looking forward, we exclaimed with delight at the peculiar richness and beauty of the picture. Below us — a thousand feet — among the evergreens at the foot of our trail rested two beautiful Alpine lakes, mirroring the blue sky and white clouds. Beyond them, was the horizon of green undulating mountains.

The Professor said the little Alpine lakes marked the birthplace of one of the main branches of the great glacier that had hollowed out Big Cottonwood Cañon. Indeed, he assured us that the névé or glacier-snow had risen a solid white wall high above the divide on which we were standing. The lakes, resting now where the snow had lain, belonged to the last page of the glacial history. Their basins, scooped out originally by the living glaciers, had only filled with water as the old glacier, pursued by the sun, withdrew up the cañon to its birth-place and there melted away. In melting, it dropped its last burden, forming dyke-like terminal moraines, which dammed the outlet of the basin and made the little lakes.

From the divide, we rode down the flowering sides of the mountain to the lakes, when the Professor sent a man back with the horses: for we were now only a short walk from "Brighton's," the stopping place at the head of Big Cottonwood Cañon, and we wanted to loiter at our pleasure along the way.

Clouds seemed to be gathering, so we hurried on to a miner's cabin among the evergreens. To our chagrin, when we got there the door was locked, the host absent, and we were obliged to sit down beside the ashes of the camp-fire.

I was getting hungry by that time, but I saw clearly that no morsel would pass the lips of the botanists till their precious plants were all a pressing; so I looked about, enjoying the streams of pure water running by the cabin, and the delicious flavor of the balsams growing over it. Then I sat down on a stump by the campfire and whetted my appetite by looking at the lunch bag.

Presently, I became aware that we were being received by the little friends of the miner — a family of ground squirrels or spermophiles — droll little creatures looking like rats with short bushy tails. They frisked about the rocks, popping up out of one dark hole to disappear down another; and then, scenting our lunch, came to see what we had brought them. Though it was wrapped in paper, inside the sack in which it had been fastened to the saddle, their keen noses led them straight to it; and before we knew it, one of them was gnawing through the sack, ignoring the fact that it lay at my friend's very feet.

This made it necessary to open the lunch, and, as the plants were safely stowed away at last, it occurred to the botanists that they, too, were mortal. We threw the little animals crumbs from our feast, and they came freely for them.

While we were absorbed in their gambols, the owner of the cabin appeared — a big burly Irishman with mild blue eyes and a patient face. He took the door key from under a tin basin, and, hospitably disregarding our having camped before his front door, began asking about the fishing. I smiled to myself at his mistaking the Professor for a fisherman.

When he opened his door I looked curiously into the cabin where we had hoped for shelter. Frying pans and other utensils were scattered over the floor, and a ragged old sheepskin hung over the edge of the rude wooden frame that served for bed — a dreary home to come back to, after a hard day's work. The lonely miner sat down on an upturned box and took up a newspaper, politely leaving us to ourselves — in his front-door yard.

When he found us watching his little friends, however, he came out. I asked him if they would come to him. Pointing to the mother, he said, "She will, she likes sugar;" and turning back into the cabin, he brought out a slice of bread thickly spread with molasses. Leaning down in the doorway he held it out, gently calling her to come for it. As soon as she heard his voice the little creature ran trotting up to her big friend, and stood by his hand licking off the syrup as confidingly as a kitten. It was a touching picture, and reminded me of the prisoner cherishing the little flower that sprang up in his window.

"Will she ever climb up on your lap?" I asked.

"Oh, sometimes, when you're sitting on a chair, she'll come up, if she's right hungry," he said.

When the Professor took a flower from his botany can and began making notes upon it, the miner's blue eyes lit up with interest. "Does every flower have a name, or do you name them?" he asked; adding something about "classifying" them, much to my surprise.

The Professor, in his turn, inquired about the miner's "claim." It was gold and silver, he said; but he was only "working out his assessment." "It does n't pay to get out silver, now," he explained quietly. Then, referring to the "silver trouble," with a force that surprised us, he exclaimed, "It takes a good deal to kill a Western man. It takes more than *one* thing to starve a Western man."

While the Professor and the miner were talking, I became interested in the pretty chipmunks that were running about the rocks. But when I asked the miner if he thought I could get them to come to me — the mother spermophile had not been afraid to take food from my hand — he declared, "You'll have a job to get them — they're too old-fashioned;" though just what fashion had to do with it, he did not explain.

Nevertheless, the Professor was plunged

deep in his notes, and the squirrels were coming near, so I took some sponge cake and thought I would try. I scattered the pieces on a log beside me, and in a few minutes a plump, frank-faced chipmunk ran up to get them. And soon, while the brown spermophiles were picking up crumbs at my feet, occasionally raising their pretty black eyes to look up at me, my pretty chipmunk answered my coaxing, and not only climbed up in my lap, but sat in one of my hands picking up crumbs, while I talked caressingly to him, stroking his soft striped fur. The astonished miner sat cross-legged in his doorway, watching. At first, I thought he showed a touch of jealousy that his pets should make so free with a stranger, but it vanished before his surprise and kindliness. "That beats anything I ever see with a chipmunk," he declared. "You've got that one pretty slick."

After my pet had eaten all he wanted, and had carried off a goodly supply of cake for a rainy day, a threatening thunder-shower started us on our way. I had waited for him to go off to his storehouse, but when I turned to look back, I caught sight of my pretty pet coming for more, with such a bright, alert expression it went hard with me to disappoint him and leave, just as we were getting to be such good friends.

The miner, when we suggested that he might become lonely, answered, with assumed indifference, that he had plenty of company; but when thanking him for his hospitality, on leaving, the sad expression settled back over his patient face, and he said gratefully that he was glad to have any one come to see him.

As we walked down toward Brighton's, he passed above us on his high trail across the mountain side going to his " claim," and at our last sight of him, he was looking down the black mouth of his tunnel, — a lonely figure on the mountain.

The Professor, who had just been collecting mining statistics, grew warm as he discussed the exaggerated expectations of miners, telling us — in figures — how little is averaged by the prospector; and how the trained miner, whose skill is greater than that of a carpenter or other tradesman, combines prospecting with his trade, so taking his hard-earned money and "blowing it all out."

We walked past the two beautiful little lakes, — typical Alpine lakes, — with grassy points running out into the clear water, suggesting feeding deer; willows growing along the banks, and great granite boulders standing in the water.

The sight of a dear homelike robin warmed our hearts as we passed, but white clouds were piling up over our heads, and we could only hurry by.

When the trail led through a grove of fir, we met a party of summer hotel young men, calling for a gun — they saw grouse in the trees. I heard them recalling their recent achievements — they had killed a badger, a deer, and an eagle within a few days. It was a rude shock to me, and I thought bitterly that even these wild grand mountains would soon be "civilized" by the pleasure-seekers who destroy all they can of the nature they come to enjoy; leaving the country lifeless and bare, after having had the refined satisfaction of taking pleasure in giving pain, of taking life to evade the tedium of an idle hour. I could only reflect thankfully that though the mountains might be made patent-medicine advertisers, and the deer that drank from the lakes at their feet and the eagles that soared over their heads might be killed to gratify man's lust of power, the cloudless blue sky above us was beyond their reach.

I resigned myself to a wetting while the botanists loitered gathering new flowers, oblivious of the drizzle; and amused myself watching the chipmunks playing among the rocks, and the humming-birds whizzing around the flowers — the hillsides seemed to whirr with them.

The situation of Brighton's is one of commanding beauty. As the Professor explained, it stands at the head of the mountain-encircled glacial amphitheatre into which the glacier from the Alpine lakes, and the other branch glaciers, came down, joining to form the great glacier that excavated Big Cottonwood Cañon. Rounded masses of rock — "roches moutonnées" — on the walls of the amphitheatre showed where the different glacier heads had come over. The whole flat bottom of the amphitheatre was formerly a lake, dammed back by a terminal moraine; but now there is only a small trout pond fed by a willow-bordered brook. All the vegetation of the place was boreal, for we had come down only about two thousand feet from the divide; and in winter the hotel is buried under twenty feet of snow.

We spent the evening over a great blazing fire, and in the morning started on our twenty-five mile stage ride back to Salt Lake City.

As we rode along, the Professor told us the geological story of the cañon. Just below the hotel we drove over a moraine two hundred feet thick. We felt as if we were in Switzerland, following along the course of the glacier with its lateral moraines left high on the mountain sides, blocking the mouths of narrow tributary cañons; its various terminal moraines marking its resting places as it withdrew up the cañon; till at last we came to the point where the sun had originally forbidden its advance, turning the river of ice to a river of water.

After that, the Professor pointed out the difference between ice-worn and water-worn cañons, enabling us to read the history for ourselves wherever we traveled. Quoting an eminent geologist on the shape of a cañon, he said, "U spells glacier; V water erosion; the resisting ice scooping out the sides of the walls, while the water cuts at the bottom." From it, a child could always recognize a glacial cañon; for, looking up or down, the Titanic U is recognized at a glance.

At the mouth of the cañon, where the river had emptied into Salt Lake, we drove past the old bar, extending like a tongue up into the cañon.

Although there is no river in the cañon now, the road follows beside a great rushing stream, for several miles of its course going over what is known as "the steps" — a series of ledges over which it leaps and foams like some exulting spirit.

The cañon itself is one of the grandest in the Wasatch. In places, towering peaks rise thousands of feet into the air, while all the cañon lines are strong and sweeping, giving an impressive sense of breadth and majesty.

Though the cañon is rich with vegetation, the only birds I remember from our clattering race down the grade were a flash of red and gold from a startled tanager; and a glimpse of a water ousel disappearing ahead of us low over his foaming stream.

We traversed the plant zones in rapid review in our descent, coming from the Alpine flora at Brighton's, past the firs of the mountain sides, to the level of oak and finally sage brush in the mouth of the cañon. Outside the cañon we entered a new world, with bright sunflowers along the fences, fields stacked with sheaves of wheat, and others busy with haymakers loading hay.

Irrigation ditches looked amazingly civilized to us now. One huge trench of pale green water on the outskirts of the city we were interested to learn was the water from the Jordan, coming from Utah Lake to supply the irrigation system of Salt Lake City.

When at last we rattled through the city streets to catch our train home, the amused smiles of the people along the way suddenly made us conscious of our mountain equipment, and our original stage with its blue and white awnings spread over each seat. But we could join in the merriment, our only regret being that we could not go back on the return trip to the mountains.

For though we had seen much in our three days, we had not had time to visit the famous Mary's Lake, declared to be equal in beauty to any Alpine lake in Switzerland.

A few weeks later, however, my brother joined me, and we made another flying trip into the mountains, climbing to the lake on horseback from Brighton's. It was a steep trail up the wall of the amphitheatre, and then alongside the smooth worn "sheep-backs," on which were patches of yellow flowers. Scattered along the trail were a number of clear little mountain lakes, one lying in a beaver meadow.

Mary's Lake has a double setting, its own smooth granite-walled basin being inclosed by the higher mountain wall. Sloping down from the lofty peaks behind it is a rock slide — a mass of broken granite blocks — a "Lagomys slide," the naturalist exclaimed exultantly; explaining that it was undoubtedly inhabited by the queer, rabbit-like creatures called "coneys" by the mountain men. Little is known about these strange animals except their remarkable habit of making hay; they gather grass and flowers, cure them on the rocks in the sun, and then store them in haycocks for winter's use. As their homes are usually in inaccessible mountain fastnesses, among broken rocks on the highest peaks, the opportunity to study them at Mary's Lake is peculiarly favorable.

We dropped from our horses, slipped the reins over their heads — the Western method of hitching — and cautiously climbed up the slide to watch for the shy coneys, whom we could hear bleating above and below us. By climbing noiselessly to a vantage ground, and keeping silent for a time, we saw a number of them. I had an exciting glimpse of one, in a crevice between two rocks only a few feet away. The pretty rabbit-like head appeared in the doorway, and to my surprise the mouth opened wide and out rang the queer bleating cry. Just then the coney caught sight of me and retreated, but I felt that I had had a thrilling experience.

When we came back to the lake, we exclaimed anew at its surpassing beauty. In its ring of glacial-rounded granite were niches that enshrined dark solemn spire-shaped evergreens. In the middle of the little lake, from the centre of its clear water rose a great granite boulder — a tiny island, also bearing spire-like firs that pointed to the sky. After our steep climb up the lonely trail with only deserted mining tunnels along the way, it seemed a step aside into a hidden sanctuary. The fresh mountain air came cool over our faces, the morning sunlight silted through the silent firs, giving a green gleam to the mountain side and touching with a tender vivid light a bit of meadow on the border of the lake. No sound broke the stillness, no ripple stirred the smooth pure face of the lake, over which arched the deep blue sky. A hush had fallen upon our spirits. It seemed as if the noble mountains under whose great shadow we had passed the summer had at last admitted us to their Holy of Holies.

www.ingramcontent.com/pod-product-compliance
Lightning Source LLC
Chambersburg PA
CBHW020304170426
43202CB00008B/494